W9-BFE-418

WITHDRAWN

TO MY LOVING PARENTS, CARLOS AND MI SU CHONGUE, WHO TAUGHT
ME THE WORLD WAS AT THE TIP OF MY FINGERS, THAT LIFE WAS SHORT
AND TO MAKE THE MOST OF EVERY MOMENT. IN EVERY JOURNEY THEY
HAVE STOOD BEHIND ME, REMINDING ME ABOUT WHO I AM.

Green

WITHDRAWN

Plants for small spaces, indoors and out

PROPERTY OF CLPL

Green

Plants for small spaces, indoors and out

Jason Chongue
From The Plant Society

Hardie Grant
BOOKS

Contents

Why plants?

I have always loved having my hands in soil. Gardening comes with a sense of calm and contentment that is hard to find anywhere else. I was lucky enough to grow up with a suburban garden, where my parents and grandparents allowed me to garden for days on end. I learnt organically, building my skill set in how to tend to a wide range of plants both indoors and out.

I was passionate about being a gardener, but I never once thought it could become my career. As children and adolescents, when we are asked what we want to be when we grow up, we tend to aspire to become doctors, lawyers, astronauts or architects, as they are notionally amazing jobs. I guess I chose to become an architect because I loved all things design, and somehow it felt more admirable than becoming a gardener. Now I question why our society undervalues such process-based careers; my evolution from architect and interior designer to plant curator has been one of the most memorable journeys of my life.

When I wrote my first book, *Plant Society*, I was also working as an interior designer. It was a role I enjoyed, but my partner Nathan and I had launched The Plant Society as a passion project that strove to connect our community of gardeners and promote sharing knowledge between local gardeners and aspiring plant enthusiasts. By the time I finished the book, we had opened our very first store in a warehouse in Collingwood, Melbourne, with the then Mina-no-ie cafe. It was an instant urban oasis that brought plants, design and modern Japanese-inspired cuisine together. Our audience increased, and we were at the tipping point where we could see The Plant Society really becoming something. I decided it was time to give it everything I had, and with the support of those around me I left my stable job to go on this crazy plant journey.

It wasn't always easy – there were days when we did not sell a single plant. I would close the store up and, on my way home, ponder how much our city needed more green.

Most of our cities were designed to include parks and greenery, where architecture sat seamlessly amongst towering trees and curated gardens. We've always found ways to bring green into our busy city lives: entry doors anchored with potted plants and leafy hidden courtyards waiting to be discovered. Such spaces bring people together, inviting comfort, connection and relaxation.

With space at a premium, we prioritise the man-made over nature. Many have forgotten how green brings life to our urban

spaces, but we crave it now more than ever. That's why it's important that we attempt to nurture greenery in our homes, retail stores, offices and apartment towers. Imagine it: plants caressing concrete boundaries, and balconies overflowing with ornamental and edible foliage, ushering nature back into our lives. It invites a sense of calm, creating a retreat where we can switch off, drowning out the city noises with the rustling of leaves.

I knew that my community needed more plants; I just wasn't sure how we could motivate people to buy them. But then I remembered a lesson from my gardening past: if things aren't going your way, change your tactics.

So we focused our efforts on education, teaching commercial clients and budding plant enthusiasts how to use plants in their spaces. It took a lot of push, but we found our way alongside architects and interior designers, helping to prove that plants could live happily in small urban spaces – that they were easy to nurture, and more rewarding than any artificial plant could ever be.

With this book, I want to give you a helpful guide to creating gardens, both indoors and out, that will enrich your home and community. From indoor spaces to courtyards and balconies, this book will take you on a guided journey, providing you with tips and simple steps so you can create your own green oasis.

Chapter 1 will help you understand your climate – the one outside your front door and the one within your home – and how to work with it instead of against it. We'll talk about how to choose the right plants for your small space, considering all the conditions and challenges that might impact your garden. Chapter 2 sets up the fundamentals of styling with plants. Chapter 3 offers a guided tour through a range of homes and public spaces where greenery plays a vital role in complementing our urban surroundings. Chapter 4 dives into the details of plant care, including how to cultivate plants and keep them looking great. Chapter 5 will help you troubleshoot when things go wrong so that you'll have a thriving urban garden in no time.

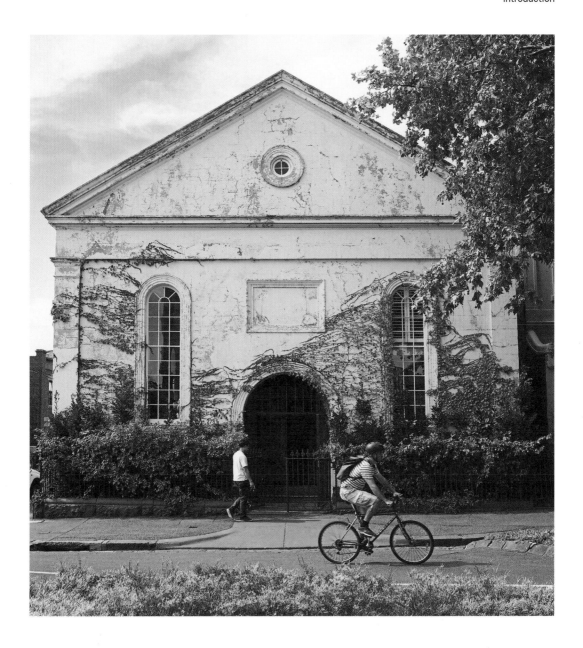

By approaching gardens in small spaces step by step, you will build up your skills and confidence to approach a range of plant species and natural conditions while understanding how to care for them.

As a child, I challenged myself by growing a range of plants. It taught me that gardening was all about practice and patience. I hope this book motivates you to extend your skills so that you can garden anywhere, experiencing many moments of green.

OPPOSITE LEFT: Indoor plants soften an entry at a blow-dry bar.

OPPOSITE RIGHT: A range of plants and handmade planters decorate The Plant Society flagship store.

ABOVE: A narrow front yard is no excuse for a lack of greenery. Try growing climbing plants and compact shrubs.

Just like plants come in an array of shapes and sizes, so too do our surroundings. When we talk about plants in our cities, we need to consider how every space is unique. Our urban spaces, both indoors and out, can influence the plants we grow. From compact plants to ones that scale facades, there will be one that's perfect for your small space.

Jason's top tips

1 PLAN WELL

When it comes to curating plants in small spaces, it pays to sit down and plan. It might include the style you envisage, how many plants you want to use and where they will go. The key is to give yourself a clear direction when sourcing plants and planters.

2 DON'T BE CHARMED BY LOOKS

We all make the mistake of choosing plants purely because of how they look, but it's more important to choose them by their lighting needs. Above all else, you want to make sure they'll work in your space.

3 KNOW WHO YOU ARE AS A GARDENER

If you're nervous about gardening, then choose plants that are easy to care for and low maintenance. Start with a handful of plants and slowly build up your garden once you get a handle on how to care for it.

4 FOCUS ON THE FUNDAMENTALS

Plants are living things. They require the fundamentals of water, light and nutrition, so keep on top of these so your plants can thrive.

5 TAKE IT SLOW

There's no rush when it comes to gardening. Don't force instant results. The plant world is on a journey of its own, so make sure to slow down and enjoy the process.

6 CARE FREQUENTLY

Plants don't thrive on neglect. Check in on them regularly: my tip is every week or two. Regular check-ins will help you monitor your plants and catch any problems early.

7 DON'T PANIC

When you have plant problems, don't freak out. Try to systematically pinpoint the problem, which will point you to the best solution. Plant diseases take time to resolve. Keep treating until the problem has disappeared.

8 SPEAK UP

Even now, I'm always asking for gardening advice. Don't be afraid to seek help from family, friends, neighbours and online plant friends.

9 BE YOURSELF

The great creatives in our communities offer us an opportunity to buy unique planters, lovingly designed or made by hand. You don't have to follow the trends; instead, use planters that you relate to.

10 ALWAYS EXPERIMENT

A great gardener always pushes their boundaries. It's great to try new species and plant types to challenge your skill set in other areas.

Chapter 1

Understanding your climate

Establishing a garden of any size can be daunting, but also extremely exciting. The fear of killing plants can be enough to prevent anyone from picking up their trowel and giving it a go.

When I begin working on an urban garden, I take note of space, sunlight and the level of maintenance required to ensure my chosen plants will thrive. Before you get started, it's important to take the time to observe how the sun moves through your space throughout the day, understand your climate conditions and be honest about how much time you want to spend in your garden.

Plants, like people, come from a range of backgrounds and prefer different conditions. Understanding these conditions will help you choose plants that are better suited for survival in your particular space. After assessing the conditions on offer, try choosing plants from the natural environment that best reflects your urban climate.

Observing natural light

Natural light is like food to plants: not enough or too much of it will directly affect how they grow. Before choosing plants for your space, observe which direction your garden is facing and how the light travels through it as the day progresses. As the sun moves, its intensity increases, reaching its height in the afternoon before setting for the day.

Take note of any shadows that fall on your space – they will offer some shelter for shade-loving plants you might want to incorporate.

With such a wide variety of plants to choose from, it's important to understand the various light conditions, and what different plants need to thrive. If you select the right plants for your light conditions, then your garden will be off to a flying start.

ABOVE: Afternoon sun and extreme light are perfect for an easy-care arid garden like this one, especially in drought-prone areas.

PICTURED (FROM LEFT): San Pedro cactus (*Echinopsis pachanoi*), pig's ear (*Cotyledon orbiculata*), prickly pear cactus (*Opuntia*), agave, spineless yucca (*Yucca elephantipes*), aloe family.

OPPOSITE: A great way to extend the atmosphere in small spaces is to continue your greenery from outside to inside. This balcony exposed to part sun leads into a dining room filled with dappled light.

PICTURED (FROM LEFT): (BALCONY) A series of cranesbills (*Geranium*), good luck palm (*Cordyline*). (INDOORS) Heart-leaf philodendron (*Philodendron cordatum*), wax plant (*Hoya*), peace lily (*Spathiphyllum*), tractor seat plant (*Ligularia dentata reniformis*).

Sunlight conditions

1 Afternoon sun/extreme light

OUTDOORS

Plants will receive direct sun during the hottest time of the day, typically around 4 pm. In extreme weather conditions, ensure plants are protected with shade cloth to prevent sunburn to foliage.

Recommended plants/varieties

The Euphorbia family, such as African milk tree (*Euphorbia trigona*) or Mediterranean spurge (*Euphorbia wulfenii*), rosemary, lavender (*Lavandula*), cabbage tree (*Cussonia spicata* or *Cussonia paniculata*), citrus, cacti, succulents, maiden silvergrass (*Miscanthus sinensis*), purple fountain grass (*Pennisetum setaceum* 'Rubrum'), olive (*Olea europaea*), geraniums, eucalyptus, grevilleas, banksias, *Ficus*, wisterias, Queensland bottle tree (*Brachychiton rupestris*), roses (*Rosa*).

INDOORS

Direct afternoon sunlight or positioned 1–2 metres (3–10 feet) from a window.

Recommended plants/varieties

Euphorbia family, most cacti and succulents.

2 Full sun/harsh light

OUTDOORS

Plants will receive at least 6 hours of direct sun per day.

Recommended plants/varieties

Maples (*Acer*), silver birch (*Betula pendula*), dichondras, lamb's ears (*Stachys byzantina*), umbrella tree (*Schefflera amate*), grevilleas, banksias, rosemary, salvia family, wormwood (*Artemisia*), *Ficus*, roses (*Rosa*).

INDOORS

Position plants close to windows that receive direct sun for most of the day.

Recommended plants/varieties

Kauri pine (*Agathis robusta*), umbrella tree (*Schefflera amate*), desert palms, most succulents and cacti.

3 Part sun/well lit

OUTDOORS

Plants will receive 3–6 hours of sun, typically during the morning or evening.

Recommended plants/varieties

Tractor seat plant (*Ligularia dentata reniformis*), hydrangeas, dichondras, Japanese aralia (*Fatsia japonica*), hellebores, salvia family, begonias, iris.

INDOORS

Position in a place that receives several hours of direct sunlight throughout the day.

Recommended plants/varieties

Begonias, fiddle-leaf fig (*Ficus lyrata*), wax plants (*Hoya*), peace lily (*Spathiphyllum*).

4 Part shade/dappled light

OUTDOORS

Plants will receive 3–6 hours of indirect sun, sheltered by buildings or larger trees and shrubs.

Recommended plants/varieties

Bromeliads, dichondras, violets, maidenhair fern (*Adiantum*), bird's nest fern (*Asplenium*), cast-iron plant (*Aspidistra elatior)*, staghorn or elkhorn ferns (*Platycerium*), Japanese aralia (*Fatsia japonica*).

INDOORS

Position in a place with indirect sunlight, sheltered by larger foliage, or 2–3 metres (6–10 feet) away from windows.

Recommended plants/varieties

Arrowhead plants (*Syngonium podophyllum*), Chinese evergreens (*Aglaonema*), prayer plants (*Maranta leuconeura*), queen of hearts (*Homalomena*), zebra plant (*Aphelandra squarrosa*), forest palms, Chinese money plant (*Pilea peperomioides*).

5 Full shade/low light

OUTDOORS

Plants will receive less than 3 hours of direct sun, usually sheltered by a larger shrub or tree.

Recommended plants/varieties

Cast-iron plant (*Aspidistra elatior*), staghorn or elkhorn ferns (*Platycerium*), Japanese aralia (*Fatsia japonica*), hellebores, violets, dichondras.

INDOORS

Position in dark spaces or rooms with minimal natural lighting or where windows are shaded by outdoor trees or obstructions.

Recommended plants/varieties

Cast-iron plant (*Aspidistra elatior*), peace lily (*Spathiphyllum*), *Philodendron*, Zanzibar gem (*Zamioculcas zamiifolia*), zebra plant (*Aphelandra squarrosa*).

6 No light

INDOORS

Positioned in spaces with no natural light. Typically, rooms with no windows.

Recommended plants/varieties

Cast-iron plant (*Aspidistra elatior*), Zanzibar gem (*Zamioculcas zamiifolia*), *Philodendron*.

Note: No plant can survive without any sun, so you'll need to rotate them – a good rule of thumb is two weeks in a spot that receives daylight, followed by two weeks in an unlit space.

It's easy to write off urban spaces as being too hard to grow plants in. Ultimately, it's about choosing wisely and making them work in the space at hand.

ABOVE: On windy balconies, try hardy plants that can withstand the harsh sunlight and exposure to the elements.

PICTURED (FROM LEFT): Star jasmine (*Trachelospermum jasminoides*), yucca.

RIGHT: When floor space is at a premium, consider using a tree and curating a cluster of plants below it.

PICTURED (FROM LEFT): Mint (*Mentha*), cumquat (*Citrus japonica*), thyme (*Thymus vulgaris*), Vietnamese mint (*Persicaria odorata*).

Considering the elements

The elements interact with our city spaces in different ways. Sometimes, our buildings deflect wind away from outdoor spaces, other times, they channel a draught. Buildings can reflect light and store warmth, depending on their orientation and colour. It's important to understand that wind and rain conditions can be positive or negative, depending on the plants within the space. When we take a look at deserts, we find cacti that have evolved to withstand extreme wind. That same wind might damage a tropical plant and put stress on it. When it comes to urban gardens, you have to choose plants that will cope with their surroundings.

When creating gardens, whether indoors or out, with plants that are not from your climate, you will need to create a microclimate for them. That means mimicking conditions from the plant's natural environment. We must become plant parents, meeting their needs in terms of rain, light, nutrition and shelter.

The effect of wind on gardens is regularly overlooked. Outdoors, on a veranda or balcony, it can sometimes be intense, causing damage to elegant, leafy plants. In this scenario it's important to provide your plants with shelter. Try to use objects, structures and even other plants to create a wind buffer. Layer your greenery, building a small network of plants that will support each other, and watch out for the drying impact of wind on soil.

Breezes indoors can be good. Allowing air to flow through your space will get rid of any stagnant air and provide your plants with fresh oxygen. If your space is lacking air flow, simply having a fan or people moving through it can create enough movement to keep the air from turning stale.

For indoor plants, you can bring rain inside simply by watering them. This, however, doesn't just mean hydrating your plants. Rainfall also helps clean foliage; it essentially gives your plants a shower so they can breathe again. If you have a suitable outdoor area, it is a good idea to give your indoor plants a proper rain shower from time to time by placing them outside (beware of sudden changes in temperature and windburn, though, as this can cause shock). Failing that, you can place your indoor plants in the shower and bathtub from time to time and carefully hose them down with the showerhead to simulate the benefits of rainfall outdoors.

Just like out in the wild, your plant's requirements depend on its natural climate and geography. The following pages dive into a few of the main climate types and offer suggestions about which plant species might work in your small space.

Arid plants

When we think about the harshest natural environments, the first place that comes to mind is the desert: expanses of barren land that experience harsh sun and extended dry periods, creating difficult growing conditions. The plants that do survive are the most amazing specimens.

They also tend to be resilient in small urban spaces, capable of dealing with harsh conditions and prolonged dry spells, and their sculptural elements add personality to any space. With a few considered green additions mixed in, you can use arid plants to turn your space into a low-maintenance garden that can survive a summer drought.

Below are a few plant varieties and species to get you started.

1 HAIRPIN BANKSIA (*BANKSIA SPINULOSA*)

2 EUKY DWARF (*EUCALYPTUS LEUCOXYLON*)

3 CASCADING ROSEMARY (*ROSMARINUS OFFICINALIS 'PROSTRATE'*)

4 SAN PEDRO CACTUS (*ECHINOPSIS PACHANOI*)

5 LAMB'S EARS (*STACHYS BYZANTINA*)

6 BIRTHDAY CANDLES (*BANKSIA SPINULOSA*)

7 EMU BUSH (*EREMOPHILA NIVEA*)

8 CROWN OF THORNS (*EUPHORBIA MILII*)

9 RED LANTERN BANKSIA (*BANKSIA CALEYI*)

ALSO TRY

Agave family, golden barrel cactus (*Echinocactus grusonii*), gum trees (*Eucalyptus*), euphorbia family, olive (*Olea europaea*), banksias, rosemary, lavender (*Lavandula*), cotton lavender (*Santolina chamaecyparissus*), geraniums, wormwood (*Artemisia*), houseleek (*Aeonium*), aloe, sea holly (*Eryngium planum*), paddle plant (*Kalanchoe*), purple fountain grass (*Pennisetum setaceum* 'Rubrum'), pride of Madeira (*Echium*), grevilleas, Jerusalem sage (*Phlomis*), Queensland bottle tree (*Brachychiton rupestris*).

Mediterranean plants

Some urban spaces experience similar conditions to the climate around the Mediterranean: think dry summers and rainy winters. These conditions can be tough for plants on balconies, exposed verandas and courtyards, so Mediterranean plants might be your best solution. During summer, the buildings around us heat up and store the sun's warmth, which in turn creates a dry climate for our urban gardens. Not many of us are fortunate enough to have time to regularly water our outdoor plants, so when choosing plants for tough conditions, you should always keep drought tolerance in mind. You want to choose a plant that will survive, not one that won't make it to the end of the week.

Some Mediterranean plants are a common sight in our city environments; there is a reason why they're used so heavily in urban spaces. They last through harsh warm weather, and when wet weather comes they spring back.

Here are a few plant varieties and species to try in your Mediterranean garden.

1 CASCADING ROSEMARY (*ROSMARINUS OFFICINALIS* 'PROSTRATE')

2 BAY TREE (*LAURUS NOBILIS*)

3 CITRUS

4 GERANIUMS

5 LAVENDER (*LAVANDULA*)

6 POPPY (*PAPAVER RHOEAS*)

7 OLIVE TREE (*OLEA EUROPAEA*)

8 OREGANO (*ORIGANUM VULGARE*)

ALSO TRY

Roses (*Rosa*), jasmine (*Jasminum officinale*), wisterias, wormwood (*Artemisia*), agave, euphorbia family, blue fescue (*Festuca glauca*), salvia family, lamb's ears (*Stachys byzantina*), yucca.

Edible plants

When working with limited space, it's a bonus when a plant looks good and offers something you can use in the kitchen. Gardens can be more than ornamental: they can also be useful in our homes and public spaces. There are a lot of edible plants to choose from, from common herbs such as thyme and rosemary to edible flowering plants such as nasturtiums and trees with useful foliage such as Kaffir lime.

Below are some practical edibles that work well in any garden.

1 OREGANO (*ORIGANUM VULGARE*)

2 CASCADING ROSEMARY (*ROSMARINUS OFFICINALIS 'PROSTRATE'*)

3 OLIVE TREE (*OLEA EUROPAEA*)

4 BAY TREE (*LAURUS NOBILIS*)

5 STRAWBERRIES (*FRAGARIA X ANANASSA*)

6 MINT (*MENTHA*)

7 ONIONS (*ALLIUM CEPA*)

8 ITALIAN FLAT-LEAF PARSLEY (*PETROSELINUM CRISPUM VAR. NEAPOLITANUM*)

9 CITRUS

ALSO TRY

Thyme (*Thymus vulgaris*), lettuce, bok choy, sage, apples, peaches, quinces, spinach, blueberries, gooseberries, tomatoes, garlic, nasturtiums.

Temperate plants

Temperate climates can be the most exciting to work with. If you're living in a city with distinct seasons, then the sky's the limit for your garden. The temperature can change greatly between the warmer and cooler months, and the plants you choose can change with them.

Harness a temperate climate's potential by integrating plants that change with the seasons. This might include deciduous plants with their changing foliage, or plants that flower seasonally. Temperate plants provide moments of excitement throughout the year, so your garden is never stagnant. You will also give yourself rewarding gardening tasks to tackle all year round.

Here are some plant varieties and species to try in a temperate garden setting.

1 LADY FERN (*ATHYRIUM FILIX-FEMINA*)

2 NORFOLK ISLAND PINE (*ARAUCARIA HETEROPHYLLA*)

3 SIKKIM CREEPER (*PARTHENOCISSUS SIKKIMENSIS*)

4 RABBIT FOOT FERN (*DAVALLIA*)

5 SILVER BIRCH (*BETULA PENDULA*)

6 MAPLE (*ACER*)

7 BOSTON IVY (*PARTHENOCISSUS TRICUSPIDATA*)

ALSO TRY

Australian natives, maidenhair
fern (*Adiantum*), maidenhair tree
(*Ginkgo biloba*), cherry blossom
tree (*Prunus pendula*).

A floral harvest

Floral plants can add so much excitement to a garden throughout the year. If planned cohesively, your urban garden will incorporate a range of shades and tones to break up all the greenery.

My tip for choosing flowering plants in small spaces is to avoid a rainbow of different colours and stick to a few shades. By choosing only shades of reds and orange, for instance, you're sure to have a seamless-looking garden.

Below are some plant varieties and species to start with.

1 DAISY (*ARGYRANTHEMUM*)

2 CROWN OF THORNS (*EUPHORBIA MILII*)

3 BIRTHDAY CANDLES (*BANKSIA SPINULOSA*)

4 EGYPTIAN STARCLUSTER (*PENTAS LANCEOLATA*)

5 CONEFLOWER (*ECHINACEA*)

6 ROSES (*ROSA*)

7 GERANIUMS

8 EMU BUSH (*EREMOPHILA NIVEA*)

ALSO TRY

Allium, iris, clivia, hippeastrum, orchids, hydrangeas, poppy (*Papaver rhoeas*).

Creating a microclimate

Our buildings aren't always designed to house gardens, but where there's a will, there's a way. The key to working with a difficult canvas is to think outside the box and plan for the future. When I moved into my home, endearingly named 'The Workers' House', our front veranda was concreted over. Facing due west, I knew the front of the house would melt in the summer and all that concrete would hold the heat overnight, often for days. I was told nothing would survive, but the thought of having a harsh entry into our home got me planning ahead. I knew I wanted a gentle dry garden that would soften the hard surfaces and welcome us home from the street. Of course, it eventually had to overflow with foliage, but initially I had to set up a microclimate: one that I could alter to suit the plants I wanted to grow.

The first plants I tried were two climbing Julia's roses. I knew they would take a couple of years to establish, so I wanted to get them in the ground right away. I also knew they would cope with the heat and grow over the veranda, keeping the floor space free for a rambling potted garden. When it comes to creating gardens in small spaces, my favourite tip is to take advantage of vertical space. Climbing or creeping plants are great for introducing a wealth of green without taking up valuable floor space. When I begin curating a garden, I approach the specimen plants – the ones that will be the most influential – first. This might be with an aesthetic approach, such as incorporating a large tree for impact, or it may be from a functional perspective, like growing vines to create shelter for yourself and your garden's more delicate foliage.

Next, I planted citrus trees and a box hedge to create shelter for the delicate plants I was to plant the following year. It worked! I had created a small enclosed garden right off the street, and as it has established over the years I've added thyme, a range of roses, rosemary and some sculptural succulents (check out the result in the image on page 65). This little retreat has given us a place to sit among the green – a place to enjoy some afternoon nibbles, or eat breakfast whilst having long yarns with our neighbours.

How to adapt to artificial seasons

In our indoor spaces, we have inadvertently created artificial seasons. We are creatures of habit that like our homes at a certain temperature all year round. Indoor heating and cooling creates a controlled environment that changes elements of our atmosphere, removing moisture from the air, drying out our skin and our plants' foliage. As gardeners, we need to work a little to combat the negative effects of these artificial seasons.

When moisture is removed from the atmosphere, we need to replace it. Misting your plants in the mornings can help prevent their foliage from going brown at the edges. You can also place a bowl of water near the heating or cooling source so that the water evaporates into the air.

Use your artificial seasons to your benefit. It might allow you to grow plants you would not have been able to grow in your natural environment. With the constant temperature, try growing rarer plants that love heat. Challenge yourself with plants such as Philippine orchid (*Medinilla magnifica*), bleeding heart vine (*Clerodendrum thomsoniae*) or red-vein maranta (*Maranta leuconeura*). If rare plants aren't for you, stick with easy-care plants that can withstand artificial heat such as devil's ivy (*Epipremnum aureum*) and peace lily (*Spathiphyllum*).

I don't expect anyone to switch off their heating and cooling to save their plants from distress; however, there are some tricks to keeping your plants thriving in temperature-controlled spaces. Choose plants that can withstand blasts of hot and cold air. It's never ideal to have your plants in this scenario, but some will battle through. Use them as a buffer, like you would outdoors. Clustering your plants and layering them in groups will create a small ecosystem: a mini plant family that will shelter each other during waves of heating and cooling.

OPPOSITE: In apartments, heating and cooling vents are often integrated close to the ceiling. Observe how the air flows through your space when you turn on your heater or air conditioner. You can minimise the effect of artificial heating and cooling on your plants by placing them a metre or two from the source.

PICTURED (FROM LEFT): Devil's ivy (*Epipremnum aureum*), mistletoe cactus (*Rhipsalis*), spider plant (*Chlorophytum comosum*).

RIGHT: If you have a split system heater and air conditioner, you may want to place your plants directly below it so the artificial air flows above and past your plants.

PICTURED (FROM LEFT): Rubber plant *(Ficus elastica)*, weeping fig *(Ficus benjamina)*.

Seasonal changes

A seasonal garden is so rewarding. I can't think of anything better than being surrounded by plants that respond to the changes in temperature and light throughout the year, altering our spaces and reminding us that we live in a natural world.

My garden is layered with deciduous plants and heirloom flowers – they bring me so much joy when they change colours. The autumn foliage on my Japanese maples serves as a reminder of the importance of rest. When the leaves change from green to red, Nathan and I begin our own season of rest and hibernation.

As the seasons shift, make sure to be conscious of how your plants respond to climatic changes, both indoors and out. It's important to remember that your gardening techniques will need to adapt to the different conditions. The major shifts you'll want to make concern water, light and temperature.

Embrace seasonal changes. When curating your outdoor garden, try incorporating deciduous plants that change colour with the seasons.

PICTURED: (LEFT) Boston ivy (*Parthenocissus tricuspidata*). (OPPOSITE) Crepe myrtle (*Lagerstroemia*), Boston ivy (*Parthenocissus tricuspidata*).

Gardening calendar

Gardening becomes easier when you're prompted to do certain tasks throughout the year. If you let the list of undone chores get out of hand, it will simply make it harder to catch up. It's not just about the growing season, but also about prepping to ensure plants have a good go at thriving when it is time for them to grow.

It's important to remember that the plants you're likely dealing with are diverse living things and have come from all corners of the globe. They are different, but they all respond to the seasons. Some lie dormant in the winter while others thrive in the cold. Some flourish in the warmth, waking up in spring and running rampant in summer. To honour your garden, whether indoors or outdoors, you need to nurture them through these yearly shifts.

Gardening is a year-round passion. There are always tasks to attend to and opportunities to appreciate your garden with fresh eyes. From pruning to meandering through your garden, make sure to spend plenty of time among your greenery.

PICTURED: (OPPOSITE) Japanese maple (*Acer palmatum*), kidney weed (*Dichondra repens*). (RIGHT) Prickly pear cactus (*Opuntia*).

Gardening calendar, from season to season

SEASON	TASKS
Spring	• Feed plants with slow-release fertiliser or organic nutrients (compost). • Fertilise plants with liquid fertiliser every 2–3 weeks (refer to packaging for dosage). • Tidy any evergreen overgrown plants and prune back branches to promote new growth (page 142). • Train and tie back stray foliage and branches (page 145). • Adjust your watering as the days grow warmer. You may need to water more frequently. • Plant summer edibles and flowering plants, either as seeds or bulbs. • Repot your potted plants into a pot one size up or refresh their potting mix by removing the top 3 cm (1 in) and adding in some nutrient-rich potting mix. You could also mix in some compost (page 162). • Add a fresh layer of mulch around planters and garden beds to retain moisture as the days become warmer (page 165). • Clean the foliage of indoor plants either by hosing them down outside or in the shower. If cleaning outdoors, be careful not to leave your plants exposed to extreme weather. • Propagate cuttings either in water or soil (page 141, 156).
Summer	• Continue fertilising with liquid fertiliser every 2–3 weeks (refer to packaging for dosage). • Prune back plants with rampant growth to keep them compact and promote branching. • Train climbing plants by attaching stray branches with twine onto a supporting structure (page 145). • Pay attention to extreme weather and shelter your plants from intense sunlight. Try using shade cloth, linen, muslin or hessian (burlap). • Water more frequently to counter extreme heat. • This will be your last chance to repot plants before the cooler weather approaches (page 149).

SEASON	TASKS
Autumn	• Remove and compost any fallen foliage to keep your garden tidy. • Collect any summer seeds from your plants so you can plant them for the following year. • Plant winter flowering plants, bulbs and seeds so your garden flourishes throughout the cooler months. • Deadhead any summer flowering plants (page 146). • This is a good time to perform a hard prune of any shrubs and trees that may have grown out of control. • Pay attention to the shorter days for your indoor plants. Rotate your plants to a brighter winter spot so they can soak up some much-needed sunlight.
Winter	• Plant deciduous trees and shrubs. • Prune deciduous trees and shrubs. • Plant spring edibles and flowering plants. • Apply organic fertilisers to deciduous trees and shrubs. • Adjust watering indoors in response to cooler weather, but also pay attention to artificial heating.

Common seasonal plant problems

There are a number of seasonal plant issues that commonly crop up in gardens, but it can be difficult to know what exactly the problem is and how to fix it. Keep an eye out for the following symptoms and use this chart to get on top of them.

Warm season

SYMPTOM	CAUSE	TIPS FOR SOLVING
Holes in foliage or ragged edges	Pest	You could have a pest eating your foliage. Check closely and remove them. Alternatively, if the pest is large, try netting.
Sticky substance on foliage	Pest	A range of pests leave behind a sticky residue. Ignoring this problem may attract other pests. Treat with organic pesticide (page 178–79).
Brown tips or edges on foliage	Dry air	Mist foliage in the morning and make sure to water adequately.
Burnt foliage	Sunburn from extreme sunlight	Leave burnt foliage until the hot weather has passed. To prevent, create some shade with a shade cloth, linen or hessian (burlap).
Leaves are wilting or droopy	Too hot	Increase watering to counter warmer temperatures.
Yellowing foliage, but leaves remain firm	Soil is lacking nutrients	Sprinkle a few pinches of Epsom salts on the soil (see page 181) or a nutrient booster to increase its quality.

SYMPTOM	CAUSE	TIPS FOR SOLVING
Leaves curl, then fall off	Most likely underwatering	Water more frequently.
Brown or light brown spots on leaves	Most likely underwatering	Water more frequently.
Leaves begin to drop rapidly	Shock	If you experience rapid leaf drop it's most likely from shock, either from moving the plant or a change in environment. Treat with a seaweed tonic (refer to packaging for dosage).
Planter has white crust on exterior	Soil medium has too many nutrients	Reduce feeding.

SYMPTOM	CAUSE	TIPS FOR SOLVING
Flowers perish quickly, or flower buds fall before opening	Underwatering	When flowers don't last as long or flower buds fall before opening, it's usually a sign of underwatering or the air being too dry. Water more frequently and mist if required.
Lack of flowering	Not enough natural light or overfeeding	Move plants to brighter sunlight and fertilise less.
Leaves have large holes or are tearing	Wind or physical contact from people or animals	If you suspect your plants are being damaged by wind, create a wind barrier. Foliage can be delicate, and human or animal contact can tear it. Be careful when handling plants.

Cold season

SYMPTOM	CAUSE	TIPS FOR SOLVING
Rotting stems and foliage	Overwatering or leaving water on foliage overnight.	Allow soil to dry out. When watering, do it in the morning.
Root rot	Plant sitting in water or watered too frequently	Aerate soil with a stake and allow soil to freely drain and dry out before watering again.
Outer foliage is soft and turns brown	Frost burn from extremely cold weather	Leave affected foliage on plant until the weather warms up.
White-to-grey powdery fungal growth found on leaves and occasionally flower petals	Powdery mildew	Spray with natural fungicide (page 181).
Leaves turn yellow and fall off	Overwatering, or for natural reasons	If you are experiencing rapid leaf drop after leaves turn yellow, try reducing your watering frequency. If the odd leaf turns yellow on the bottom, this is normal.
Leaves are small and plant is leggy	Not enough light or underwatering	Check to see if the soil is overly dry; if so, water more frequently. If there is a lack of light, move the plant to another position.

Plant People

Kristen Pumphrey and Thomas Neuberger

P.F. Candle Co.

Los Angeles, United States

OCCUPATION: CEO & CREATIVE DIRECTOR /
COO & SALES AND OPERATIONS MANAGER

HTTPS://PFCANDLECO.COM/ @PFCANDLECO

TELL US HOW YOUR LOVE FOR CANDLES CAME ABOUT.

Kristen: My mom has been a serious candle burner for as long as I can remember. My sister made candles for a Home Ec fair in middle school, and after she was done with the kit I 'inherited' it (little sister speak for 'stole it') and started making candles in the kitchen. I was around 12. I made candles throughout high school and college for fun, and then when I wanted to start a handmade business it seemed only natural.

Tom: The easy answer is from Kristen. She's made candles the entire 10 years I've known her. The complicated answer is I really like the history and the mechanics behind it. For most of human history, candles were the only source of indoor light we had. How people were smart enough to make a self-contained lamp out of animal fats is insane!

YOUR SCENTS RELY ON THE NATURAL WORLD. HOW HAS THIS CHANGED OR STRENGTHENED YOUR IDEAS ABOUT NATURE?

Kristen: Nature is the best perfumer, and we draw so much inspiration from plants when it comes to our scents. My favorite weekend activity is strolling through a herb garden (The Natural History Museum here in Los Angeles has an incredible one) and touching all the plants.

Tom: With scents, I think about the chemicals that break down to create them. Most of the stuff from nature shares common compounds like thymol, and it gives them similar scent notes.

YOUR RANGE IS SEAMLESSLY CURATED WITH PLANTS. HOW HAVE PLANTS AFFECTED THE RETAIL ENVIRONMENT?

Tom: Plants in the retail environment are a net positive. They help reduce our carbon footprint and purify the air for us. In our shop, not only do customers get greeted by great scents, but the air quality is probably a bit better than what they just experienced outside it.

Kristen: Tom said it best here! When we thought about setting up our shop, I looked to our own home: what did we have and enjoy already? Plants are not only beautiful, but serve a function.

WERE YOU AN AVID GARDENER BEFORE P.F. CANDLE CO.?

Kristen: Probably not. I don't think I developed my green thumb until we moved to California. I had access to the flower market here (we lived a block away) and just went nuts. I'm the indoor gardener in our house, and Tom's the outdoor gardener.

Tom: I wouldn't say I was an avid gardener before we moved into our current house. I never had the space to grow things. Now one of the things I enjoy most in the world is working with the land. Tending to the garden, terracing our soil, just trying to be a good shepherd of what we have.

HOW HAS NATURE INFORMED YOUR BUSINESS?

Tom: We are natural beings, so it makes sense to look to nature for guidance. What company structures work well in nature? How do people communicate best with each other? We also care deeply about the environment. My goal is to reduce most of our packaging to just the items themselves. It is extremely frustrating when you put so much time and resources into something and people just throw it away.

Kristen: Like Tom said, part of what motivates us is being able to make an environmental difference from a corporate standpoint. I felt frustrated by my limitations as an individual – yes, I can make responsible choices, but it's a much smaller impact than corporations can make. I truly believe they have the biggest responsibility when it comes to climate change. Something I'm proud of is that we've started composting here at P.F. HQ. We also want to put solar panels in.

HAVE THERE BEEN CHALLENGES WITH HAVING PLANTS IN YOUR STORE?

Kristen: Watering can be an issue. We have a great patio, so we'll rotate them out there for a nice shower. And they'll get little yellow leaves if they don't have perfect sunlight. I'll usually trim these off for customers before I send them home.

Tom: Trying to keep them alive is a challenge, but I think it's one our shop peeps enjoy.

WHEN CREATING NEW SCENTS, HOW DOES NATURE FACTOR INTO IT?

Kristen: We just love starting with natural inspirations (like cedar) and pumping it up with other notes to make it really full-bodied. We also think about a sustainable approach for the fragrance industry going forward. We have an all-natural line and a man-made/natural blend line. There are limitations to the type of aromas we can create with all-natural scents, because some items are cost prohibitive in their natural form and some are outright banned (like musk: you can't get that natural). I believe that man-made fragrances are a sustainable way forward for the industry, because they put less strain on our natural resources. For example, it takes 48 kilograms (105 pounds) of rose petals to make 5 mL of rose essential oil. These are so highly concentrated, and I don't think their best use is for fragrance candles. We use essential oils lightly for that reason – to round out a scent rather than be the entirety.

Tom: For us, a lot of time the scent-building process starts in a botanical garden, asking what nature put together that works already, or what two scents people might love to experience together that aren't together already.

Chapter 2

Styling with plants in your space

At The Plant Society, we specialise in curating spaces with plants. It's more than just selecting plants we like: rather, we focus on continuing the design language of the place, extending every detail into the plants we choose and allowing our clients' personalities to carry through. It's their space to enjoy, after all, and we love designing spaces that reflect our clients' desires.

To many, a plant is just a plant. But to us, every one has a different personality. When we go about curating a space, we look closely at how intricate a plant's foliage is, how deep its green, and we think about what its scale and texture might bring to an environment. Always, our plant selections are guided by what will thrive in the climate at hand. We want our plants to continue giving back, not turn into lifeless stumps.

When curating your own spaces, take note of the materials you already have to work with and use them to inspire the plants you select. Observe tones and colours, letting them influence the planters and plants you choose. Coupled with the right planters, plants will quickly add life to any space, help to ground furniture and change the atmosphere. What follows are some styling tips and rules of thumb to help guide your decisions about what plants to buy and ensure they thrive no matter what sorts of small urban spaces you're working with.

Harnessing your canvas

When it comes to curating urban spaces, it certainly doesn't have to be on trend, expensive or mass produced. I love drawing inspiration from what is already on site, complementing the history of the space or reinterpreting it so that it breathes your personality.

So don't run out and buy blindly. The first thing is to catalogue your space's hero pieces: things like furniture, artwork, sculptures and existing planters. Then pinpoint materials in your space that you already love: an old brick wall, for instance, or an aged concrete floor. Whatever it is, if it triggers a positive emotional response, then it is something you want to celebrate. It's easy enough to create a look, but creating atmosphere takes time and a certain eye.

Once you have taken note of objects and materials you love, keep them in mind when you're plant or planter shopping. You might be in love with an aged concrete floor, which will help guide you in choosing planters that have a concrete finish or a bold black to complement the neutral colours in your space. Next comes the plants: if you're after a minimal look, then try using large-foliage plants like fruit salad plant (*Monstera deliciosa*) or large succulents like agave.

MATERIALS AND TEXTURES I LOVE:

Brick walls

Render

Concrete

Natural metals

Timbers

This small, moody bathroom (RIGHT) uses two considered plants to soften the hard concrete and terrazzo. Their delicate foliage adds a softer touch to what is a rigid space. Notice how the fine foliage textures capture light and shadow, adding depth to the room.

PICTURED (FROM LEFT): Leatherleaf fern (*Rumohra adiantiformis*), dragon tree (*Dracaena marginata*).

For bland and lifeless spaces (FAR RIGHT), try incorporating colourful plants with a range of leaf sizes. The deep-purple foliage of this elephant ear stands proud among the dense rose foliage and strappy, variegated spider plant.

PICTURED (FROM LEFT): Spider plant (*Chlorophytum comosum*), elephant ear (*Colocasia*), roses (*Rosa*).

Layering to create an urban landscape

My favourite cities around the world all incorporate a balance of beautiful planting and refined architecture. From the lushness of The High Line in New York City to the creepers that scale London's buildings, a city is more appealing when plants and architecture intertwine to form a layered urban environment.

Nurturing plants in small spaces is no different than curating parks on a larger scale: it's all about layering. In nature, you find different plants growing among one another to create a more lush and interesting whole. Planting in clusters will help you create your own unique foliage layers.

Quick tips for styling with plants

PLANT IN ODD NUMBERS

When curating planters and plants, try to work with odd numbers when creating potted landscapes. They are typically easier on the eye and flow better.

CONSIDER HIERARCHY

Always anchor the space by giving some elements the spotlight, then add plants that will work well in a supporting role. This, in turn, will create a layered garden and will allow you to incorporate a mix of textures.

CREATE A CONTINUOUS LANGUAGE

It is easy to get carried away in small urban spaces by using too many colours, textures and plant species. To avoid your space becoming too busy, limit yourself to a few colours or textures. To achieve a continuous language, I often use planters in the same finish and only a handful of plant species.

ADD TEXTURE

This is one of my favourite design elements to harness. Using texture when styling, whether through foliage or planters, can add so much character to a space. Observe how ruffled foliage can catch the light and shadow, adding depth and intricacy. Steer away from your typical hardware store planters and embrace the work of local ceramicists, which will bring a unique touch to your space.

PLAY WITH SCALE

To avoid your space looking monotonous and flat, incorporate plants in a range of sizes so that larger and smaller plants complement one another.

GET SEASONAL

We forget that gardens can look great all year round, even in the cooler months. Think about how your garden will present itself throughout the seasons (page 38–42). Certain plants thrive in cooler months, while others thrive in warmer months.

UNDERPLANTING

Whether potted or in a garden bed, finish your garden with some interesting underplanting: in other words, incorporate smaller plants underneath larger ones. Creeping or clumping plants are great for this as they provide a dynamic canvas for overflowing foliage.

LET NEIGHBOURS INSPIRE YOU

You don't have to feel nervous about starting your urban oasis. We often forget we live in a community, so take a stroll around your neighbourhood or have a chat with your neighbours to see what plants are working for them.

Useful styling and growing props

There are many tools and props out there to help you on your gardening journey. The options below are tried and tested, and handy when it comes to shaping and arranging plants.

TRELLISES

If you want your plants to climb up walls, trellises provide the perfect support and help guide them as they grow.

ARCHES

Growing arches allow you to train your plants into an interesting form and add a nice architectural element to your garden.

POT FEET

They add a touch of character, but pot feet also raise your planters off the floor so they can drain freely, which prevents moisture build-up.

STAKES

Top-heavy and wind-sensitive plants tend to need a helping hand. Stakes are an easy way to provide instant support for taller plants or flower spikes.

WIRE

You will need to secure stray branches from time to time. Wire is a great long-term solution. If you do not have wire, try using twine or string.

PAINT

A dash of paint can go a long way when introducing character to your garden. Painting your planters can make a standard pot, or even an old one you already have lying around, look completely different.

CHAIN

If you want to suspend plants from the ceiling or a structure, then make sure to use chain.

Playing with form, texture and colour

When curating small landscapes, the most interesting ones are accentuated by a range of colours, textures and plants of various scales. Plants have their own personalities, so try and complement or juxtapose them.

Here are a few to try, shown from top to bottom, left to right.

AFRICAN MILK TREE (*EUPHORBIA TRIGONA*)

A thick, green-stemmed succulent covered in thorns and teardrop-shaped leaves.

SALVIA FAMILY

Commonly found in country gardens; however, this woody plant variety is great for small urban spaces as well. Seasonally, the plant is covered with tubular flowers on small spires.

POLKA DOT PLANT (*HYPOESTES PHYLLOSTACHYA*)

Small, heavily patterned and coloured leaves make the polka dot plant great for introducing texture to any garden.

ECHIUM FAMILY

To best appreciate their jaw-dropping sculptural qualities, it's best to give plants in the echium family room to breathe. Not only are their leaves architectural, but when their flowers emerge, they can tower above all.

THYME (*THYMUS VULGARIS*)

An aromatic herb useful in everyday cooking and perfect for planting along paths, where they can release their fragrance when people brush past.

JAPANESE ARALIA (*FATSIA JAPONICA*)

Large, glossy leaves provide a solid backdrop for privacy purposes, and are great for planting at the back of garden beds or in pot clusters.

RABBIT FOOT FERN (*DAVALLIA*)

Named for its furry aerial rhizomes, which grow on bark or rocks. Its delicate fern fronds make it an elegant choice in internal courtyards or pots where you can see them up close.

WAX PLANTS (*HOYA*)

These trailing or creeping vines come in a range of glossy leaf forms, textures and colours. With a myriad of varieties, they all grow well on trellises or cascading from hanging planters.

GRAPEVINE (*VITIS*)

As the seasons change, the grapevine's foliage changes colours. In autumn, it puts on a beautiful show, turning yellow and bright red.

HIMALAYAN CEDAR (*CEDRUS DEODARA*)

Adorned with blue needles and a weeping aspect, the Himalayan cedar has a nice irregular form. It often grows lopsided, making it a great feature plant for both large pots and in the ground. If you're up for a challenge, try bonsaiing the Himalayan cedar.

HYDRANGEAS

Famous for their classically formed flowerheads, hydrangeas display immense seasonal colour.

BLOODLEAF (*IRESINE HERBSTII*)

If you're after bright foliage, the bloodleaf is a great choice.

WANDERING JEW (*TRADESCANTIA ZEBRINA*)

A creeping plant that creates a lush ground cover either indoors or out. Be sure to keep it under control as it is a prolific self-propagator.

DEVIL'S IVY (*EPIPREMNUM AUREUM*)

The perfect shelf plant for small indoor spaces. Allow the foliage to cascade over hard edges. This highly cultivated plant is quite versatile as it adapts well to low and bright light.

WATERMELON PEPEROMIA (*PEPEROMIA ARGYREIA*)

Famous for its watermelon-like foliage, this radiator plant suits tabletops or shelves indoors.

FIRE STICKS (*EUPHORBIA TIRUCALLI*)

This low-care desert plant grows into a large succulent shrub with vivid foliage. It's great for dry and harsh light environments.

PASSIONFRUIT (*PASSIFLORA EDULIS*)

This vining plant grows rapidly and bears exotic produce adorned with glossy foliage. Plant it along your fence line or balcony.

CABBAGE TREE (*CUSSONIA SPICATA* OR *CUSSONIA PANICULATA*)

Less commonly found in gardens, but well worth the hunt. Heads of textured foliage stand boldly on gnarly trunks.

SPOTTED VIETNAMESE ASPIDISTRA (*ASPIDISTRA EBIANENSIS*)

Much like its plainer cousin the cast-iron plant (*Aspidistra elatior*), the spotted aspidistra is low-maintenance and perfect for shadier positions.

MAIDEN SILVERGRASS (*MISCANTHUS SINENSIS*)

Predominantly grown for its soft, airy flowers, the maiden sivergrass's graceful foliage provides a delicate touch to any space.

FLOWERING GUM (*CORYMBIA FICIFOLIA*)

Growing into larger specimen trees, flowering gums produce nectar-rich flowers that form gum nuts as the flowers fade. Grow these in full sun where they can soak up the natural light.

JERUSALEM SAGE (*PHLOMIS*)

Its felt-like foliage adds a softer touch to any drought-prone position.

ROSES (*ROSA*)

There are a vast variety of roses with different growth habits, colours and sizes. Some see roses as a bit old fashioned, but they look beautiful when grown among other plants such as citrus and Australian natives. They often require similar watering conditions, and their texture helps give a garden depth.

SMOKE BUSH (*COTINUS COGGYGRIA*)

Soft, fluffy flowers and deep maroon or green foliage make the smoke bush the perfect plant for picking flowers or foliage for cut flower displays.

BAY TREE (*LAURUS NOBILIS*)

Grown as an aromatic shrub, this large plant is a great alternative for topiary and hedges, and its leaves can be used for seasoning in cooking.

HELLEBORES (*HELLEBORUS*)

Cultivated for their vast variety of cup-shaped flowers, these clumping plants are great for underplanting.

SPIDER FLOWER (*GREVILLEA* FAMILY)

Predominantly grown for its brush-like flowers, the spider flower also has an array of textural foliage types.

MISTLETOE CACTUS (*RHIPSALIS*)

This rainforest cactus family presents a wide variety of leaf forms. Perfect as an underplanting in shady spaces, or indoors on tabletops, shelves and hanging from the ceiling.

LAVENDER (*LAVANDULA*)

Lavender grows well in a variety of places. Try planting outside in pots as a border or cross-planted with vegetables.

Plant combinations

Typical urban spaces are hard-edged and barren. Plants add atmosphere to concrete, stone and timber, bringing any space to life. After shortlisting plants that will survive in the natural light and elements provided by your space, it's time to experiment with plant textures, colour and growth habit. Choosing the right plant combination is key to curating a seamless garden with character.

CREATING POTTED LANDSCAPES

Planting directly into the ground in urban spaces is not always an option, but this shouldn't deter you from creating a lush garden of your own. Potted plants can easily come together to create their own garden.

Just like in any landscape, there are a few key principles that bring together a good potted garden. Carefully positioning and nurturing a group of plants can create a calming backdrop. I prefer to position a group of potted plants together, allowing them to grow wild over time. In a controlled, man-made environment, it's nice having foliage sweep over structured materials.

I like to incorporate a specimen plant: when used alone, it becomes a statement plant that anchors any space and becomes a focal point. When used in a cluster with other plants, it can help ground the whole collection. Usually it's a larger, more established plant, or one that has an interesting shape: something a little gnarly or a tree with unique foliage.

Plant combinations grouped according to climate

When pairing plants, it helps to select a handful that require similar lighting and watering conditions. Here are some plant combinations that go well together.

Plant combination 01 – A temperate courtyard

It's easy to overpopulate small courtyards with too many plant types. For a simple aesthetic, limit yourself to three types and plant them in multiples. Try using a tall plant or tree, a shrub and a ground cover. Here's an example of a combination that works well when creating a temperate courtyard.

Plant varieties and species (from right):

SILVER BIRCH (*BETULA PENDULA*)

When limiting yourself to three plant types, you want to incorporate a large specimen – the hero plant that people will notice first. Its graceful nature and silver-toned bark make silver birch a great centrepiece. In autumn, its foliage turns bright yellow, creating drama as the weather cools down.

CASCADING ROSEMARY (*ROSMARINUS OFFICINALIS* 'PROSTRATE')

Drawing inspiration from the silver birch's delicate foliage, we'll use rosemary as an intermediate shrub. Introducing cascading foliage allows for a better connection between the planter and the plant, grounding your garden and filling the space under your hero tree without competing with it. Perfect for dry gardens, its flowing growth adds fragrant foliage to potted planters.

DICHONDRA 'SILVER FALLS' (*DICHONDRA ARGENTEA*)

Lower down, the dichondra 'Silver Falls' continues the silver tone from our hero tree, creating a textural, tonal carpet of foliage. It's great as a ground cover, cascading over pots and overflowing from hanging planters.

Plant combination 02 – A dry garden

Curating larger garden beds can be intimidating, so try using a range of plants that can adapt to dry conditions. As a fan of dry, almost wild planting, I love the following combination with its strong layering of textures. Even if left to grow wild, they will turn into a striking garden bed.

When you are selecting a larger range of plants for your space, take note of what colour the flowers will be and how you can play with a mix of foliage colours and textures. Here, I've paired the deep red and burnt orange tones across the rose, coneflowers and crown of thorns. Focusing on this detail allows your garden to speak the same language.

To incorporate visual drama, put light foliage with dark. The combination of lavender and emu bush creates lighter foliage pockets when planted among the roses and coneflowers.

Plant varieties and species (from left):

LAVENDER (*LAVANDULA*)

With its soft grey foliage, this low-growing shrub makes a hardy plant that can handle hot summers. With its dense growth, it creates nice borders or can be clipped into topiary balls in pots. It comes in a variety of species that flower at various times of year.

EMU BUSH (*EREMOPHILA NIVEA*)

An Australian native shrub that bears beautiful silver foliage and purple tube-like flowers. It doesn't like humidity, so is well suited to drier environments.

SIKKIM CREEPER (*PARTHENOCISSUS SIKKIMENSIS*)

This creeping ground cover will finish off any garden bed with its deep-green, delicate leaves.

CONEFLOWER (*ECHINACEA*)

The coneflower provides an attractive flower head in a multitude of colours.

CROWN OF THORNS (*EUPHORBIA MILII*)

A flowering succulent adorned with spiky stems that form dense shrubs.

ROSES (*ROSA*)

You can't pass a rose without admiring its beauty. Try planting roses in corners or allow them to creep up wires to bring bursts of colour in the warmer months.

Plant combination 03 – A dry accent

For those wanting a few potted accents, even simple additions can add life to a neglected corner. If you are looking for something low maintenance, stick to arid or Mediterranean plants. They withstand short periods of harsh weather and bounce back with a little bit of love.

Plant varieties and species (from top):

OLIVE TREE (*OLEA EUROPAEA*)

This drought-tolerant shrub or tree is perfect for pots and planted in the ground. Its silver foliage and gnarly nature make for an interesting feature plant or privacy screen.

PADDLE PLANT (*KALANCHOE*)

I recommend pairing the olive tree's delicate foliage with a visually heavier plant. The paddle plant (or any similar succulent) makes mounds of large, plump foliage that add visual weight to your garden.

Plant combination 04 – An indoor trio

If you're worried about ending up with a rampant indoor jungle, try starting with a clustered trio. Think about height and scale: how tall your plants will grow and how much space you want to fill and soften.

Plant varieties and species (from left):

DRAGON TREE (*DRACAENA MARGINATA*)

The height of the dragon tree in this trio will fill a corner perfectly. It has elegant, long leaves and is hardy too, storing water in its trunk so it can withstand long periods of drought.

MISTLETOE CACTUS (*RHIPSALIS*)

These rainforest succulents often bear flowers and can be planted as underplanting in pots, sitting on shelves or cascading from hanging baskets.

BLUE STAR FERN (*PHLEBODIUM AUREUM* 'BLUE STAR')

A uniquely blue-foliaged plant with large, hand-like fronds.

Away from the typical

Nature is phenomenal, and plant choices are almost limitless. With a wider range of plants available all the time, try to experiment with intriguing specimens that are less familiar to you. Less common plants add interest while sometimes challenging your gardening skills. Below are good options to experiment with.

SAN PEDRO CACTUS (*ECHINOPSIS PACHANOI*)

A statuesque cactus that provides a strong architectural element. *Also try*: Spurge (*Euphorbia ammak* or *milii*), blue torch cactus (*Pilosocereus arures*).

EMU BUSH (*EREMOPHILA NIVEA*)

An Australian native shrub bearing beautiful silver foliage and purple tube-like flowers. It does not like humidity, so is suited to drier environments. *Also try*: Pink paper bells (*Guichenotia macrantha*).

DICHONDRA 'SILVER FALLS' (*DICHONDRA ARGENTEA*)

Adorned with silver foliage, 'Silver Falls' is great for a range of spaces. It's great as a ground cover, cascading over pots and overflowing from hanging planters. *Also try*: Dichondra 'Emerald Falls', donkey tail (*Sedum morganianum*), sedum 'Blue Feather'.

NORFOLK ISLAND PINE (*ARAUCARIA HETEROPHYLLA*)

Bearing soft green needles in a typical conical tree form, the Norfolk Island pine makes the perfect hardy specimen for any potted garden or garden bed. Give it enough room to grow and it will tower in your garden. *Also try*: Monkey puzzle tree (*Araucaria araucana*), kauri pine (*Agathis robusta*).

CASCADING ROSEMARY (*ROSMARINUS OFFICINALIS* 'PROSTRATE')

Excellent for dry gardens, its cascading growth adds fragrant foliage to potted planters. *Also try*: String of beans (*Senecio radicans*).

BIRTHDAY CANDLES (*BANKSIA SPINULOSA*)

With its compact and dense growth, this dwarf banksia is perfect for small gardens. Its brush-like flowers attract an array of wildlife and make a sensational display. *Also try*: Scarlet banksia (*Banksia coccinea*).

PONYTAIL PALM (*BEAUCARNEA RECURVATA*)

An unusual specimen with long, draping foliage that grows from a large, bulbous trunk. *Also try*: Dragon tree (*Dracaena marginata*).

HEDGEHOG CACTUS (*ECHINOPSIS*)

Growing in clumps of prickly orbs, these are easy-care plants that will fill any planter over time. These sun lovers throw out some sensationally bright flowers that last for short periods. *Also try*: Pigface (*Carpobrotus*).

BLUE STAR FERN (*PHLEBODIUM AUREUM* 'BLUE STAR')

It offers unique blue foliage with large, hand-like fronds. *Also try*: Bear's foot fern (*Aglaomorpha meyeniana*), staghorn or elkhorn ferns (*Platycerium*), button fern (*Pellaea rotundifolia*).

Plant People

Lucy Wise
Tamago

Wellington, New Zealand

OCCUPATION: DESIGNER

HTTPS://TAMAGO.CO.NZ/ @TAMAGO_DESIGN

HOW MANY PLANTS ARE IN YOUR COLLECTION?

Around 12 to 18.

TELL US ABOUT YOUR JOURNEY TO BECOME A CERAMICIST.

My ceramics journey started back in 2015 when I was immersed in an architecture PhD and was looking for a way to reconnect design with the art of making. The tactility and sculptural qualities of clay made it a natural choice, as did the history and durability of ceramics. To think that ceramic objects are some of the oldest-known human artefacts is incredibly compelling! The medium connected with many design principles I had been exploring through architectural design – form, structure, context, function, surface treatment etc. Now I think of myself more as a designer using clay as a means of creative expression than a ceramicist exploring the technical aspects of clay.

YOU MAKE EXQUISITE PLANTERS. WHY PLANTERS, AND WHAT INSPIRES THEIR FORMS?

I've made many different types of vessels, but always seem to come back to planters. I'm always looking for a strong personality and sense of playfulness in my designs. All my planter prototypes to date have

been driven by one of two design considerations: the relationship between the planter and the drip tray, or the way the planter relates to the surface on which it sits. I try to imagine the spaces where my planters might end up and work to create statement pieces for those spaces.

WHEN YOU MADE YOUR FIRST PLANTER, WHAT CONSIDERATIONS DID YOU KEEP IN MIND?

I didn't know much about indoor gardening when I started making planters. The designs I initially produced were quite shallow and fully glazed, some without drainage holes. Over time I've learnt how important soil volume, drainage and the ability for the material to breathe is, so I rarely glaze the inside of planters and always make sure they have drainage holes. When I first experimented with ceramic planters, I was trying to understand the strength of clay; how much weight it could support and what might happen when slightly precarious forms were fired at very high temperatures. Many of these prototypes collapsed in the kiln, but after some refinement, eventually these experiments led to the design of the three-legged planter now called the Tamago Planter.

YOU RECENTLY HAD A NEW ADDITION TO YOUR FAMILY. HOW HAS THIS INFLUENCED YOUR PRACTICE?

Life is reasonably chaotic at the moment, juggling work with family commitments. My husband is very involved with Tamago too. While I physically make the products myself, we spend countless hours together discussing new designs, manufacturing methods and business opportunities. Our daughters, Poppy (2) and Frida (1) are growing up surrounded by cardboard models, 3-D printed prototypes and an ever-growing collection of ceramic planters and indoor house plants.

Having a young family has taught me the real value of time. Tasks have to be prioritised and everything is now done with a lot more intent. My design process has definitely changed to accommodate the reduced hours I have in the studio. I now spend more time designing through thinking, sketching and model making, so that when I do get into the studio I have a clear vision for what I am about to make.

WHAT EXCITES YOU ABOUT YOUR STUDIO AND YOUR HOME?

My studio and home are one and the same. I have a small workspace under our house with a kiln, a potter's wheel and space for sketching and model making. Our house is in an inner suburb on the edge of the Wellington Town Belt. We love living here, so close to the city, while being surrounded by beautiful native bush and the diverse birdlife it attracts.

HOW HAVE PLANTS BECOME A PART OF YOUR LIFE?

Like many indoor plant enthusiasts, my plant journey started out with popular plant species originating from rainforest environments: fiddle-lead fig (*Ficus lyrata*), swiss cheese plant (*Monstera deliciosa*), snake plant (*Sansevieria trifasciata*), mostly because of their availability. But lately I have become really interested in collecting native New Zealand plants. We now have a small but growing collection of natives, including kōwhai and horoeka (lancewood).

Chapter 3

Creating your urban oasis

When curating your indoor or outdoor garden, it's important to make it an extension of your personality. It needs to relate to you, not just something you saw in a magazine. I always observe plant textures and growth habits and relate them back to the design elements in your space. These elements are ones that you relate to, so it should extend to the plants and planters you choose. For example, if you want to add some character to your space, you might choose a tree that is gnarly or windswept, looking much like it would growing in the wild. On the other hand, for a cleaner look, you might select a plant that is perfectly formed and symmetrical. But you also need to think about the space your garden is going to grow in: its size and conditions, its feel and flow. This chapter walks you through different types of urban spaces, from private balconies, courtyards and entrances to public office spaces, cafes and shops. It will guide you through the needs and challenges inherent in each type of space alongside examples of beautiful, flourishing gardens worthy of emulation that are sure to inspire you to get started creating your own.

Balconies

Balconies are often neglected spaces, left bare for drying clothes. To me, they make the perfect small-space garden. Being literally at your doorstep, balconies make convenient canvases for growing both ornamental plants and edibles.

The key to balcony gardens is providing your plants with shelter. Balconies are extremely exposed, so tend to turn into wind tunnels, and recieve a lot of extreme sunlight. But if you can break through these conditions, you'll have the perfect little oasis. Creating a balcony garden will make your home feel like a retreat.

When setting up your balcony garden, you'll want to consider space. The typical balcony has a limited floor area, and I would recommend saving some space for furniture so you can sit among your oasis. Try anchoring the corners of your balcony with larger planters, then tier down from there. It's nice having some larger specimens that build height and shelter your interior from extreme weather. Balconies tend to lend themselves to arid or temperate plants, which have evolved to deal with wind and dryness, and there is a myriad of plants from the desert and the Mediterranean that work well.

Use the bones of your balcony to inspire your planting. Balcony balustrades are often ugly, but they make the perfect trellis for climbing plants or hanging planters. If you have a ceiling to work with, try hanging baskets of foliage that will eventually cascade to form a leafy wall.

Plants like succulents, citrus, olive, rosemary and Australian natives are drought tolerant, making them great choices for a balcony. If your space is narrow, try growing African milk tree (*Euphorbia trigona*), San Pedro cactus (*Echinopsis pachanoi*) and espalier fruit trees. They can all be compact growers and make great tall plants for empty corners.

A heritage balcony

Older balconies are imbued with layers of history, which can challenge you to use plants you might not have considered. This balcony incorporates plants such as geraniums, taking you back to a time when flowering plants were revered – a perfect pairing for this heritage building. The balcony embraces its exposed nature, using drought-tolerant plants. Incorporating plants both outdoors and in makes this narrow balcony feel larger, while also providing intimate pockets to sit and ponder.

LIGHT CONDITIONS: (BALCONY) PART SUN / WELL LIT; (INDOORS) PART SHADE / DAPPLED LIGHT

PICTURED: (BALCONY PLANTER BOX) Yucca, cranesbills (*Geranium*), good luck palm (*Cordyline*), foxtail agave (*Agave attenuata*). (BALCONY POTS) Egyptian starcluster (*Pentas lanceolata*), daisy (*Argyranthemum*). (INDOORS) Devil's ivy (*Epipremnum aureum*), fruit salad plant (*Monstera deliciosa*), dumb cane (*Dieffenbachia*), wax plant (*Hoya*), peace lily (*Spathiphyllum*), tractor seat plant (*Ligularia reniformis*).

GROWING TIP

Populating your garden doesn't need to be expensive. Geraniums and succulents are easily propagated. Simply trim branches from a mother plant and plant them straight into soil (page 141).

STYLING TIP

If floor space is at a premium in your home, try cultivating plants on windowsills and in planter boxes. This allows foliage to overflow without compromising on space. And don't be afraid of having your garden grow against windows. Doing so can make the perfect green escape.

In a monochromatic space, extend the neutral tones by using planters made from similar or natural materials. Using neutral tones will keep your space calm and avoid colours clashing.

An apartment balcony

With plenty of morning light, this balcony celebrates an arid aesthetic: one that would still thrive if underwatered or exposed to intense summer sun. The taller plants closest to the balustrade protect the smaller plants below. Small gardens are all about balance, achieved here with a mix of larger plants positioned at the corners and a series of smaller-scale pots and plants to soften the edges. The cacti and aloe form rigid silhouettes, while the lamb's ear and spider plant add softness.

LIGHT CONDITIONS: PART SUN / WELL LIT

PICTURED: (FROM LEFT) Golden barrel cactus (*Echinocactus grusonii*), lamb's ear (*Stachys byzantina*), cacti, tree aloe (*Aloidendron barbarae*), dragon tree (*Dracaena marginata*), spineless yucca (*Yucca elephantipes*), aloe, spider plant (*Chlorophytum comosum*), radiator plant (*Peperomia obtusifolia*).

Poolside

Everyone dreams of a poolside garden party. Imagine swimming laps or lying poolside amongst a lush tropical paradise. Curating plants around your pool can effectively frame out the concrete jungle around you.

Often exposed to extreme light, swimming pools aren't the most nurturing spaces. So it pays to select hardy plants that can work with intense conditions. This pool presents a mix of tropical- and dry-climate plants accustomed to long summer days and rough winds.

As seen here, using plants such as palm trees, gum trees, grapevines, bird of paradise, Boston ivy and yucca help frame the pool organically and give it the feel of a tropical oasis. Foliage fills every corner, allowing for pockets to lie or sit in peace. Without these plants, this pool would just be a barren expanse of concrete.

LIGHT CONDITIONS: FULL SUN / HARSH LIGHT

PICTURED: (OPPOSITE, IN FOREGROUND) Grapevine (*Vitis vinifera*); (IN BACKGROUND) Cocos palms (*Syagrus romanzoffiana*), gum tree (*Eucalyptus*).
(BELOW) Boston ivy (*Parthenocissus tricuspidata*), foxtail agave (*Agave attenuata*).
(RIGHT) Bird of paradise (*Strelitzia nicolai*), spineless yucca (*Yucca elephantipes*), gum tree (*Eucalyptus*).

Courtyards

Courtyards are a luxury when it comes to small-space living. If you're lucky enough to have one, then make sure you're making the most of it! Why not create a secret garden to charm your guests when they come over for dinner?

Lush courtyards create the most beautiful screens. I like to treat them as breathing spaces: a chance to balance out your indoor space. Courtyards are often shielded by buildings, blocking valuable light. When curating a sheltered courtyard, try using a mix of hardier tropical plants, arid plants and temperate plants that prefer shade.

Use plants to balance out a lot of concrete or tiling, or train plants to create seasonal arbours that provide shelter in the warmer months. The urban courtyard is often flat and dominated by hard surfaces, so I always try to bring in a range of textures to soften masonry, concrete and facade timbers.

When it comes to harsh facades or fences, try growing climbing plants like climbing fig (*Ficus pumila*), Virginia ivy or creeper (*Parthenocissus quinquefolia*), or Boston ivy (*Parthenocissus tricuspidata*). They'll scale your building, but with the right care and pruning you'll have a green facade with the power to take you on a mini escape when you need it.

A rental courtyard

In small courtyards, try integrating unique planters to create some interesting layers. Here, bright planters visually lift what was a drab space, and relating the planters with the furniture creates a playful courtyard rather than a concrete shell. The plants are well chosen for the conditions: the umbrella tree and Japanese aralia are sheltered by the eaves, while the star jasmine is positioned along the perimeter, ensuring it receives enough light to allow it to thrive and soften the look of the brick wall as it climbs. Styling with compact plants means there is still plenty of room for the children to play.

LIGHT CONDITIONS: (AGAINST BLACK WALL) PART SUN / WELL LIT; (UNDER EAVES) PART SHADE / DAPPLED LIGHT

PICTURED: (FROM LEFT) Star jasmine (*Trachelospermum jasminoides*), Japanese aralia (*Fatsia japonica*), umbrella tree (*Schefflera amate*), lamb's ear (*Stachys byzantina*).

STYLING TIP

A lick of paint can quickly and inexpensively make your rental home your own.

GROWING TIP

When plants are positioned under solid structures or even tree canopies, don't forget to keep on top of watering and check on them regularly.

A city courtyard

This inner-city courtyard is the perfect example of what a courtyard can be when you're living in small spaces. With a lack of constant sunlight, a space only big enough for you to stand in and gridded mesh as your flooring, the best advice is to approach your garden as a potted landscape and keep it simple. Here, you will notice the use of simple white planters and accents of vintage pots, ensuring your courtyard doesn't feel chaotic. Compact plants like these introduce softness to the hard enclosure while being able to thrive in a space with part shade. Don't forget to look up for opportunities to hang plants so they can cascade downwards, which is a good way of bringing more greenery into a tiny space.

LIGHT CONDITIONS: PART SHADE / DAPPLED LIGHT

PICTURED: Arrowhead plant (*Syngonium*), dichondra 'Silver Falls' (*Dichondra argentea*), grape ivy (*Cissus* 'Ellen Danica').

STYLING TIP
Populating a tiny courtyard with greenery can help bring life to adjacent rooms by providing something naturally beautiful to admire.

An urban backyard

If you're lucky enough to have a backyard, challenge yourself with a range of plant varieties to give your garden depth and layers. With its aesthetically heavy facade, this urban courtyard balances edible produce with ornamental plants to help shelter its residents from the harsh summer sun. The purpose-built arbour will guide the deciduous grapevine to create a green ceiling, providing shelter in the summer and allowing sunlight through during winter. The raised planter box allows herbs and edibles to be easily harvested and tended to. Exposed to full sun, the Mediterranean herbs, grapevine and rose are all happy.

LIGHT CONDITIONS: FULL SUN / HARSH LIGHT

PICTURED: Assorted herbs, English ivy (*Hedera helix*), grapevine (*Vitis vinifera*), roses (*Rosa*).

A wild courtyard

Often, a solution to the rigidity of city living is to have a less manicured garden: one that is wild at heart, incorporating less structured and more temperate plants that change with the seasons. This rambling courtyard borrows landscapes from its neighbours, making it appear larger than meets the eye.

Using deciduous trees like this forest pansy adds a hero to your garden – something that commands attention. Below it and in the garden beds are a mix of foliage colours and textures, creating aesthetic highs and lows. From the soft palette of the dichondra 'Silver Falls' to the darker tones of the climbing fig, we are made to appreciate the variation in foliage.

LIGHT CONDITIONS: PART SUN / WELL LIT

PICTURED: (ABOVE) Salvia family, forest pansy (*Cercis canadensis* 'Forest Pansy'), dichondra 'Silver Falls' (*Dichondra argentea*), Japanese maple (*Acer palmatum*), purple fountain grass (*Pennisetum setaceum* 'Rubrum'), star jasmine (*Trachelospermum jasminoides*), climbing fig (*Ficus pumila*). (RIGHT) Water lily (*Nymphacea*), dwarf golden sweet flag (*Acorus pusillus*).

STYLING TIPS

Painting your fence a dark shade can make it visually disappear, letting the garden take centre stage.
Why not incorporate a water feature if you have the space? There are an array of water plants that will thrive in a potted water feature.

89

Porches, entrances and hallways

I find an entrance surrounded by plants and interesting greenery creates the most inviting welcome. It provides an insight into the home's residents and creates a gentle atmosphere when viewed from the street.

Potted plants on either side of the door are like the warmest handshake and make an easy entranceway addition. Just make sure to select the right combination of planter and plants. After all, you want them to make a statement. I tend to choose beautiful old planters with patina because I like how they create a connection to the past. When it comes to entranceways, make sure to consider access: you want to ensure your plants don't take up too much space, but will still have an impact. Try planting citrus in large specimen planters or cluster a range of succulents and cacti.

Try planting specimens with an array of underplanting, layering plants and playing with height and cascading textures. If you have room, arrange a few different planters together in a cluster. If you are a fan of perennials, underplant with seasonal flowers and tier them into your planters. Seasonal plants will allow your entry to change and greet guests with a surprise throughout the year.

Great options for outdoors are roses (*Rosa*), citrus, olive (*Olea europaea*), salvia family, poppy (*Papaver rhoeas*), purple fountain grass (*Pennisetum setaceum* 'Rubrum'), aloe, dichondras, succulents and cacti. For hallways, try devil's ivy (*Epipremnum aureum*), peace lily (*Spathiphyllum*), Zanzibar gem (*Zamioculcas*) and San Pedro cactus (*Echinopsis pachanoi*).

A potted welcome

There is nothing more inviting than potted plants to anchor your entry. To me, an entry is more than the front door: it extends into your interior, blurring the line between the outdoors and indoors. When it comes to curating plants for your entry, try using a cluster. A range of plant varieties grouped together will create a more impactful welcome.

Outdoors, choose hardy plants like succulents, arid and Mediterranean varieties. If you have a garden bed in your front yard, then hedges and screening plants will offer some privacy: buffers between your home and the surrounding neighbourhood. Indoors, choose compact plants that won't take up the hallway and will thrive on typically low-light conditions.

LIGHT CONDITIONS: (BELOW LEFT) DAPPLED LIGHT;
(BELOW RIGHT) AFTERNOON SUN / EXTREME LIGHT;
(OPPOSITE) PART SUN / WELL LIT

PICTURED: (BELOW LEFT) Macho fern (*Nephrolepis biserrata* 'Macho'), devil's ivy (*Epipremnum aureum*).
(BELOW RIGHT) Lavender (*Lavandula*), hairpin banksia (*Banksia spinulosa*), snake plant (*Sansevieria trifasciata*), cascading rosemary (*Rosmarinus officinalis* 'Prostrate').
(OPPOSITE) Olive tree (*Olea europaea*), jade plant (*Crassula ovata*), spineless yucca (*Yucca elephantipes*), foxtail fern (*Asparagus densiflorus* 'Myersii'), ponytail palm (*Beaucarnea recurvata*), pinwheel aeonium (*Aeonium haworthii*).

STYLING TIP
Use patterned planters to break up the green tones between your plants.

GROWING TIP

Don't be afraid to prune your plants back. Doing so
promotes denser, more compact growth.

A charming facade

You can't help but fall in love with this gnarly garden oozing charm. This heritage home seamlessly interacts with the plantings, making sense of every recess and architectural detail.

In keeping with the building's history, resilient geraniums are dotted throughout. These drought-tolerant plants can withstand harsh conditions and put on a regular floral show as they soak up the sunlight. It also boasts a bit of a flashback to gardens of the '50s to '70s, home to old favourites like citrus, yuccas, prickly pear and bluewoods, all of which are easy to maintain and have adapted to unforgiving climates.

LIGHT CONDITIONS: FULL SUN / HARSH LIGHT

PICTURED: (OPPOSITE TOP) Cranesbills (*Geranium*), citrus, spineless yucca (*Yucca elephantipes*), foxtail agave (*Agave attenuata*), good luck palm (*Cordyline*).
(OPPOSITE BOTTOM) Cranesbill (*Geranium*).
(BELOW) Citrus, wormwood (*Artemisia*), frangipani *(Plumeria)*, pride of Madeira (*Echium*), prickly pear cactus (*Opuntia*).

Staircase greenery

Staircases are often left bare, but a plant or two will make this transient space feel less vacant. Simply introducing greenery near a staircase will make you appreciate the quieter moments in your home or workplace. Staircases often have dappled light or low light, so I recommend choosing plants such as devil's ivy and peace lily that can withstand low-light conditions.

Try incorporating plant stands to lift your foliage off the floor; if you tuck them in corners they won't be in the way when you are running up and down the stairs. Plus, raising smaller plants off the ground will allow you to appreciate them more.

LIGHT CONDITIONS: DAPPLED LIGHT

PICTURED: (OPPOSITE) Devil's ivy (*Epipremnum aureum*), peace lily (*Spathiphyllum*).
(BELOW LEFT) Peace lily (*Spathiphyllum*), devil's ivy (*Epipremnum aureum*).
(BELOW RIGHT) Peacock plant (*Ctenanthe*).

STYLING TIP
Plant stands don't have to be purpose made. Try using interesting stools to prop your plants up.

An indoor oasis

I have a soft spot for indoor gardens; my home is filled to the brim with plants. As they scale shelves and walls, they seem to take on a life of their own. Whether in your home or office, plants can increase productivity and reduce your chances of getting sick. I find just the process of gardening extremely therapeutic.

I lean towards tropical plants, as the conditions in our home are best suited to a tropical indoor oasis: it's sheltered, warm and it provides a range of lighting conditions, much like a tropical rainforest. Tropical plants make perfect indoor plants, as they tend to adapt to the climate at hand. Not all homes lend themselves to a tropical oasis, though. Some are more suited to arid plants, as they get hot and dry in summer. Those wanting a low-maintenance indoor garden will definitely want to adopt some arid plants – they can thrive even with minimal care.

Try layering arid with tropical plants, experimenting with different textures (keeping in mind the different watering requirements for the plant types). Arid plants are perfect for bright to harsh light, while tropical plants will work in a range of positions depending on the species.

Tropical plants like fruit salad plant (*Monstera deliciosa*), devil's ivy (*Epipremnum aureum*), umbrella tree (*Schefflera amate*), dragon tree (*Dracaena marginata*) and mistletoe cactus (*Rhipsalis*) make great easy-care plants for spaces that are well lit or have dappled lighting. For extreme or harsh light, try growing succulents and cacti as they are better accustomed to intense lighting and warm conditions.

The Workers' House

With over 400 plants in our home, The Workers' House has definitely become an indoor oasis. Throughout our home, you'll find a range of vintage, handmade and unique planters that I've collected over time. For me, home is an extension of who I am; rather than trying to mimic another interior, I'm always looking for things that express my aesthetic. Many of our plants began as cuttings from family and friends, while others I've hunted down through growers and collectors.

If, like me, you find comfort in an indoor jungle, give your indoor garden a sense of order. Dedicate corners, display units, windowsills and tabletops to your plant collections. Focusing your plants in certain spaces will keep them from taking over liveable areas.

STYLING TIP
Wall shelves are perfect for smaller collections of plants.

LIGHT CONDITIONS: DAPPLED LIGHT

PICTURED: (LEFT) Watermelon peperomia (*Peperomia argyreia*), coin leaf peperomia (*Peperomia polybotrya*), Chinese money plant (*Pilea peperomioides*).
(BELOW RIGHT) Cissus tuberosa, zygocactus (*Schlumbergera*), peacock plant (*Ctenanthe*), vanilla orchid (*Vanilla planifolia*), wax plant (*Hoya*).
(OPPOSITE TOP) African milk tree (*Euphorbia trigona*), *Philodendron*, mistletoe cactus (*Rhipsalis*), mini monstera (*Rhaphidophora tetrasperma*), radiator plant (*Peperomia*), dwarf umbrella tree (*Schefflera arboricola*).
(OPPOSITE BOTTOM LEFT) Fruit salad plant (*Monstera deliciosa*), prayer plant (*Maranta leuconeura*), asparagus fern (*Asparagus setaceus*).
(OPPOSITE BOTTOM RIGHT) Chinese money plant (*Pilea peperomioides*), radiator plant (*Peperomia*), wax plant (*Hoya*), Brazilian edelweiss (*Sinningia leucotricha*), elephant's foot (*Dioscorea elephantipes*), mistletoe cactus (*Rhipsalis*).

LIGHT CONDITIONS: WELL LIT

PICTURED: (LEFT) Grape ivy (*Cissus* 'Ellen Danica'), green flame fern (*Microsorum punctatum*), peace lily (*Spathiphyllum*), macho fern (*Nephrolepis biserrata* 'Macho'), devil's ivy (*Epipremnum aureum*), arrowhead plant (*Syngonium*).
(ABOVE) Mistletoe fig (*Ficus deltoidea*), macho fern (*Nephrolepis biserrata* 'Macho'), dwarf umbrella tree (*Schefflera arboricola*).
(OPPOSITE) Umbrella tree (*Schefflera amate*), peace lily (*Spathiphyllum*).

Indoor accents

Even if your home has a simple palette like the pictured apartment, moments of green can accentuate its minimal nature quite nicely. Adding a layer of greenery has given this home an organic touch.

The white and oak planters visually disappear, preventing them from competing with the space. For this sun-drenched apartment, plants such as umbrella tree, grape ivy and macho fern are happy absorbing the day's sunlight. If you want a larger specimen plant to fill a space, an umbrella tree is a nice way to go.

STYLING TIP

Think about your interior holistically and find places to integrate your plants and furniture. For example, try using bench seats as plant stands while also leaving room to perch yourself.

Colour play

Colour, whether in planters or objects, can quickly bring life to any interior. Try investing in a good shelving unit for your objects and plants. Open shelves are great for displaying art, ceramics and, of course, plants. Over time you'll have a wall of interesting pieces.

LIGHT CONDITIONS: DAPPLED LIGHT

PICTURED: (LEFT) Devil's ivy (*Epipremnum aureum*), zanzibar gem (*Zamioculcas zamiifolia*), foxtail agave (*Agave attenuata*).
(TOP) Japanese aralia (*Fatsia japonica*), first aid plant (*Aloe vera*), dwarf umbrella tree (*Schefflera arboricola*).

STYLING TIP

Use furniture to help train your plants. As this devil's ivy (*Epipremnum aureum*) grows, winding it onto the lamp will keep it out of the way.

GROWING TIP

Propagate cuttings in water or interesting vessels. It's an inexpensive way of building up your collection or adding new varieties.

Inner-city living

For the young professional, long days at work mean our homes need to feel like an escape – somewhere we can truly relax. Plants help calm and purify the air, grounding our homes and making them feel peaceful.

Devil's ivy, spider plant and kentia palms are all good for purifying the air. Start with these, then branch out to other plants you enjoy. Try mixing tropical with arid plants to create a varied aesthetic.

LIGHT CONDITIONS: WELL LIT

PICTURED: (BOTTOM LEFT) Devil's ivy (*Epipremnum aureum*), tree aeonium (*Aeonium arboreum*), spider plant (*Chlorophytum comosum*), coin leaf peperomia (*Peperomia polybotrya*), mistletoe cactus (*Rhipsalis*).
(BOTTOM RIGHT) Kentia palms (*Howea forsteriana*), bird's nest fern (*Asplenium*), aloe.

STYLING TIP
　Place plants behind furniture to bring life to dull corners.

GROWING TIP

When plants are placed in low light, it is a good idea to rotate them into brighter positions once in a while. This will give them an extra boost.

STYLING TIP

Side tables are great for elevating your plants so they are more balanced in the room.

A textured living room

We spend a lot of time in our living rooms. These spaces should be intimate, much like this one rich with textures. The pictured room typically receives low light with pockets that range from dappled to well lit. The devil's ivy drapes from the mantelpiece, happy to withstand the lower light levels further back in the room. On the other hand, the peacock plant is perfectly placed within a pocket of light.

In a texture-rich interior, try adding lush textures and patterns through foliage. The marbled variegation of the devil's ivy, the intricate foliage of the macho fern and the patterned foliage of the peacock plant complement the rest of the interior.

LIGHT CONDITIONS: DAPPLED LIGHT TO WELL LIT

PICTURED: (OPPOSITE) Japanese aralia (*Fatsia japonica*), devil's ivy (*Epipremnum aureum*), macho fern (*Nephrolepis biserrata* 'Macho'). (ABOVE) Peacock plant (*Calathea orbifolia*).

Bathrooms

Bathrooms don't have to be an afterthought; you can easily integrate plants that accentuate your level of calm. If you have a perfectly humid environment, your tropical plants will love the microclimate. Plants that will enjoy your bathroom include peace lily, wax plant, *Philodendron*, palms and ferns.

STYLING TIP
Pause and think about how mirrors can reflect views in your space. You might find yourself appreciating plants in the reflection.

LIGHT CONDITIONS: (OPPOSITE) DAPPLED LIGHT; (LEFT) LOW LIGHT; (ABOVE) WELL LIT

PICTURED: (OPPOSITE) Wax plant (*Hoya*), peace lily (*Spathiphyllum*).
(LEFT) Leatherleaf fern (*Rumohra adiantiformis*).
(ABOVE) Spineless yucca (*Yucca elephantipes*), rubber plant (*Ficus elastica*), umbrella tree (*Schefflera amate*), peace lily (*Spathiphyllum*), bangalow palm (*Archontophoenix cunninghamiana*), lacy tree philodendron (*Philodendron bipinnatifidum*).

Bedrooms

Bedrooms are a place where we recharge, and I couldn't think of a better spot for greenery. As we sleep, the plants help to purify the air. Not all bedrooms are expansive, so if it's compact you'll want to think about places where plants won't take over the room. Try perching them on your bedside table or bedhead. Alternatively, style them in corners or alongside furniture such as bench seats. Choose plants like snake plant or cacti that won't grow horizontally and take up valuable space.

LIGHT CONDITIONS: WELL LIT

PICTURED: (LEFT) Leatherleaf fern (*Rumohra adiantiformis*), old man cactus (*Cephalocereus senilis*). (BELOW) Dwarf fiddle leaf fig (*Ficus lyrata* 'Bambino'), Japanese aralia (*Fatsia japonica*). (OPPOSITE) Peace lily 'Domino' (*Spathiphyllum* 'Domino'), snake plant (*Sansevieria trifasciata*).

STYLING TIP
Integrate objects like books with your planting to make your space more cohesive.

A shopfront home

Increasingly, we find creatives working and living in the same space, which can be challenging when you want to switch off from work. Plants can help. Curate them so they're lightly spaced throughout your work quarters and personal quarters. Just make sure to keep your studio or workspace relatively free so you can focus. There is no doubt that working for yourself means you're time poor, so try some easy-care plants like succulents, cacti, fruit salad plant and rubber plant.

GROWING TIP

Terracotta planters are porous, meaning they allow air through the side of the planter. As a result, your plants will dry out faster. Choose plants like cacti, which won't mind their roots drying out.

LIGHT CONDITIONS: (OPPOSITE) DAPPLED LIGHT; (ABOVE) WELL LIT

PICTURED: (OPPOSITE) Macho fern (*Nephrolepis biserrata* 'Macho'), fruit salad plant (*Monstera deliciosa*).
(ABOVE LEFT) Rubber plant (*Ficus elastica*).
(ABOVE RIGHT) Assorted cacti and succulents, blue star fern (*Phlebodium aureum* 'Blue Star').

Plants in public spaces

Green urban spaces shouldn't be limited to our homes. We spend a lot of time in public spaces: offices, shopping centres, cafes, restaurants and retail stores. But they're often completely devoid of greenery. Think of all the places in our cities that lie unused or without any hints of nature. If every building in the world incorporated just a little greenery, our urban environment would become something exceptional.

At twenty-one, like most Australians, I decided to pack my bags and head to the other side of the world. My curiosity about architecture and landscape led me to London, and I later spent eighteen months backpacking through Europe, Africa and India. Going from historically architectural cities like London to the middle of Malawi made me realise the importance of nature and the impact of our surroundings on our communities. That maybe we didn't need the newest gadget to make us smile, but instead real relationships with each other and our natural environment.

In recent years, we've seen cities revitalising dead urban spaces, like The High Line in New York City. Having been fortunate enough to visit The High Line in both winter and summer, I experienced firsthand how much this urban garden connects the city back to nature, allowing it to breathe and providing its residents an escape in what is one of the busiest places in the world. There are so many underutilised spaces in our cities: all we need to do is approach them from a different angle and introduce plants that will thrive within them.

Complementing your space

I often get asked about the most effective way to style public spaces, both indoors and out. My response is always a mix of styling accessories and plants. Why plants? Next time you're near a public space exploding with greenery, stop and observe as people walk by. Their response is always some mix of awe and enlightenment, a sense of contentment and calm.

Curating plants in public spaces requires a refined attention to detail. For me, it's the small things that have the biggest impact. I adore shopfronts with plants that press up against the glass and that grow so well they hit the ceiling. Imagine offices filled with greenery, providing fresh, purified air for the long days at work. Plants are often the last thing we consider when designing public spaces, but it's important that they are seamlessly integrated into any space. There is nothing worse than a black plastic pot sitting awkwardly at an entry or greeting point. Treat plants as you would any other design element, carrying the language from the materials in your space through to the plants and planters you select.

To create a seamless space, both indoors and out, it's vital to stick to some key elements, much like a painter would stick to a certain palette. Some spaces will fall naturally into a particular design style and others will need you to choose one that expresses your persona. Once you establish an aesthetic, put together a style guide: a visual board of what you like in terms of materials, colours and furniture. Use it to help guide your decisions when curating all elements of your space. Ask yourself questions like: Will this leaf texture be calm and simple, like the minimalist chair I've chosen? Or you might think: My space is bland and I want to add some texture. Let's try some interesting foliage, for instance with a Sago palm (*Cycas revoluta*).

Try to keep your plant and planter selections simple and complementary to wall, floor and furniture materials. By creating a style guide, your styling additions will become conscious decisions rather than whatever strikes you at the time. It's important to harness the aesthetic of the space you are working with to make it cohesive.

Working with plants in public spaces

Selecting plants for public spaces requires a slightly different approach to residential settings. Public spaces often see high traffic, offer less natural light and can have poor air flow.

Much like at home, choosing the right plants for the environment at hand is a critical step in ensuring they thrive.

Below are some important points to consider.

Low light

Public spaces like offices, retail stores and restaurants typically present poor lighting conditions. In a low-light scenario, pay close attention to how much natural light your space receives and where the sunlight hits. Place your plants in the locations that receive the most light, even if it isn't much.

Sometimes, spaces receive no natural light at all. This doesn't mean you have to resort to artificial plants. Instead, choose hardy low-light plants and rotate them every week or two to spaces with exposure to natural light. We like to call this a 'plant conveyor belt', where plants continuously move throughout a space to ensure they get the light they need.

Recommended plants/varieties

Note: Plants will need to be rotated into natural light every two weeks or so and should be kept in the lit position for two weeks.

OUTDOORS AND INDOORS

Cast-iron plant (*Aspidistra elatior*), Zanzibar gem (*Zamioculcas*), *Philodendron.*

Harsh light

When it comes to external public spaces, they are often exposed to extreme sun, which can lead to scorching. It's important to select plants that are suitable to dry, arid conditions. Think about species from the desert or Australian outback: plants that survive in these climates have evolved to withstand harsh sun. If you want to grow plants that need some shelter, try incorporating large trees or shrubs that will protect them. Alternatively, use shade cloth or linen to shield sensitive plants from intense sunlight.

Recommended plants/varieties

OUTDOORS

Maple (*Acer*), silver birch (*Betula pendula*), dichondras, lamb's ears (*Stachys byzantina*), umbrella tree (*Schefflera amate*), grevilleas, banksias, rosemary, salvia family, wormwood (*Artemisia*), *Ficus*, roses (*Rosa).*

INDOORS

Kauri pine (*Agathis robusta*), umbrella tree (*Schefflera amate*), desert palms, most succulents and cacti.

Poor ventilation

Public spaces often struggle when it comes to good air circulation and ventilation, which can lead to pests and diseases. In poorly ventilated spaces, try using plants with thick foliage, or those that creep along the ground. They can often withstand strong drafts, but they also don't get stressed when the air is still. Make sure to open doors and windows whenever possible to bring some fresh air in.

Recommended plants/varieties

OUTDOORS

Cast-iron plant (*Aspidistra elatior*), Japanese aralia (*Fatsia japonica*), dichondras, violet, *Ficus*.

INDOORS

Cast-iron plant (*Aspidistra elatior*), Zanzibar gem (*Zamioculcas*), devil's ivy (*Epipremnum aureum*), heart-leaf philodendron (*Philodendron cordatum*), peace lily (*Spathiphyllum*).

High traffic

When your plants are exposed to large numbers of people, the foliage is often damaged by curious fingers. Avoid using delicate foliage plants and experiment with sturdy ones that can withstand, or deter, human interaction.

Recommended plants/varieties

OUTDOORS

Most cacti and succulents, olive (*Olea europaea*), purple fountain grass (*Pennisetum setaceum* 'Rubrum'), maiden silvergrass (*Miscanthus sinensis*), rosemary.

INDOORS

Cast-iron plant (*Aspidistra elatior*), devil's ivy (*Epipremnum aureum*), snake plant (*Sansevieria*), *Philodendron*, peace lily (*Spathiphyllum*).

Heating and cooling

We love our indoor temperature at a comfortable level, but artificial heating and cooling can affect plant growth and create unsightly blemishes on foliage. If distancing your plants from vents isn't helping, then it's a good idea to choose hardy plants that can take more of a beating.

Recommended plants/varieties

Cast-iron plant (*Aspidistra elatior*), devil's ivy (*Epipremnum aureum*), snake plant (*Sansevieria*), *Philodendron*, peace lily (*Spathiphyllum*).

A curated range of plants for different spaces

In a perfect world, we'd grow plants in all of our public spaces. But sometimes, this is easier said than done, especially when you don't know where to start. When styling with plants, it helps to understand the space you're working with and know how to style it effectively. The last thing you want to do is choose the wrong plants and have them die not long after planting them.

Using plants in urban spaces doesn't need to be difficult or overcomplicated. It's often the simple tips, like these, that help the most.

Offices

Many of us spend a large portion of our time at work – too much, some would say – so why do our offices often look so lifeless? Plants in your workspace are aesthetically pleasing among the sea of filing cabinets and white desks, but they also have the added benefit of purifying the air. They help clean up that recycled air your colleagues have already inhaled, lowering your chances of becoming ill and making you happier in the process!

In the office, try using a series of plants on all surfaces to create a workspace jungle. In my opinion, the more the merrier.

Recommended plants/varieties

Fruit salad plant (*Monstera deliciosa*), cast-iron plant (*Aspidistra elatior*), devil's ivy (*Epipremnum aureum*), snake plant (*Sansevieria*), *Philodendron*, peace lily (*Spathiphyllum*), spider plant (*Chlorophytum comosum*).

LIGHT CONDITION: WELL LIT

PICTURED: Weeping fig (*Ficus benjamina*), kentia palm (*Howea forsteriana*), mistletoe cactus (*Rhipsalis*).

GROWING TIP

This highly exposed window receives extreme light, making it perfect for an arid garden.

An office on show

With a shift in how we work, the traditional office has evolved to breathe a sense of design for both staff and clients to enjoy. We are constantly reassessing work culture and thinking about how certain elements can make our workspaces more effective and efficient. The vision of a traditional office – a sea of desks – is changing, and more people are planning them with plants in mind.

We make sure to pre-select plants that will survive in the spaces we curate. Seen here, our plant selection allowed us to integrate plants into storage units, where they could attach onto walls and climb, or into seating benches to create a blur between plants and furniture.

LIGHT CONDITIONS: (TOP LEFT) WELL LIT; (TOP RIGHT) EXTREME LIGHT; (OPPOSITE) DAPPLED LIGHT

PICTURED: (TOP LEFT) Devil's ivy (*Epipremnum aureum*), heart-leaf philodendron (*Philodendron cordatum*), macho fern (*Nephrolepis biserrata* 'Macho').
(TOP RIGHT) Mistletoe cactus (*Rhipsalis*), tree aloe (*Aloidendron barbarae*), heart-leaf philodendron (*Philodendron cordatum*).
(OPPOSITE) Mistletoe cactus (*Rhipsalis*), devil's ivy (*Epipremnum aureum*).

Designer offices

Designers' offices all have their own aesthetic, but they all benefit from a considered plant approach. Look for details like colour palette, what types of furniture there are and where planters might complement the interior styling. Introducing plants is often about softening a man-made interior, so look for opportunities to give a visual break and soften masses of furniture or an expansive wall.

STYLING TIPS

Plants around your entry can make it more welcoming for clients.
Use small tabletop planters on meeting tables to bring a comfortable aspect to meetings. Instead of a mass of objects and styling props on bookshelves, try using one or two types of cascading plants to make an impact.
Desk plants can make your workspace more pleasant. Use colour to tie in with artwork or materials you might have in your office.

GROWING TIP

If your office has no natural light, try using low-light plants and rotate them into a space with natural light every fortnight.

LIGHT CONDITIONS:
(OPPOSITE, TOP AND BOTTOM)
WELL LIT; (RIGHT, TOP AND
BOTTOM) DAPPLED LIGHT

PICTURED: (OPPOSITE, TOP)
Dwarf umbrella tree (*Schefflera arboricola*),
grape ivy (*Cissus* 'Ellen Danica'), arrowhead
plant (*Syngonium*).
(OPPOSITE, BOTTOM) Peace lily
(*Spathiphyllum*), macho fern (*Nephrolepis
biserrata* 'Macho'), devil's ivy (*Epipremnum
aureum*), Japanese aralia (*Fatsia japonica*).
(TOP RIGHT) Devil's ivy (*Epipremnum
aureum*), heart-leaf philodendron
(*Philodendron cordatum*).
(BOTTOM LEFT) Devil's ivy
(*Epipremnum aureum*).
(BOTTOM RIGHT) Rubber plant
(*Ficus elastica*), pilea 'Silver Sprinkles'
(*Pilea libanensis*), devil's ivy 'Frosty'
(*Epipremnum aureum* 'Frosty'), wandering
jew (*Tradescantia pallida*), macho fern
(*Nephrolepis biserrata* 'Macho').

Cafes and restaurants

Plants bring so much life to cafes and restaurants. They make the perfect focal point or backdrop to the empty, harsh spaces we once filled with artwork and menu boards. Try using plants as a buffer between tables to make the room more intimate for patrons. If you are short on space, try utilising shelves to adorn with greenery. Adding plants to noisy spaces can also help reduce sound from echoing and bouncing off hard surfaces.

Recommended plants/varieties

Umbrella tree (*Schefflera amate* or *arboricola*), fruit salad plant (*Monstera deliciosa*), peacock plant (*Calathea*), cast-iron plant (*Aspidistra elatior*), devil's ivy (*Epipremnum aureum*), snake plant (*Sansevieria*), *Philodendron*, peace lily (*Spathiphyllum*), spider plant (*Chlorophytum comosum*).

LIGHT CONDITIONS: DAPPLED LIGHT / PART SHADE

PICTURED: (BELOW) Fiddle leaf fig (*Ficus lyrata*), umbrella tree (*Schefflera amate*).
(OPPOSITE TOP LEFT) Mistletoe cactus (*Rhipsalis*), string of beans (*Senecio radicans*), Boston fern (*Nephrolepis exaltata*), spider plant (*Chlorophytum comosum*).
(OPPOSITE TOP RIGHT) Assorted citrus and herbs.
(BOTTOM RIGHT) Boston fern (*Nephrolepis exaltata*).

GROWING TIP
Planters filled with herbs allow you to harvest fresh produce for the kitchen.

Shops

In a world of fast fashion and trends, it's a relief to see live greenery of all sorts in our shops. It highlights products and creates not only a physical break between them, but a mental breather as well. Small- to medium-sized plants make great breaks between installations, while larger specimens can anchor bare corners.

Recommended plants/varieties

Umbrella tree (*Schefflera amate*), swiss cheese vine (*Monstera adansonii*), devil's ivy (*Epipremnum aureum*), snake plant (*Sansevieria*), *Philodendron*, peace lily (*Spathiphyllum*), radiator plants (*Peperomia*).

LIGHT CONDITIONS: (OPPOSITE TOP LEFT AND ABOVE) WELL LIT; (OPPOSITE TOP RIGHT) DAPPLED LIGHT; (OPPOSITE BOTTOM LEFT) LOW LIGHT

PICTURED: (OPPOSITE TOP LEFT) Devil's ivy (*Epipremnum aureum*), fruit salad plant (*Monstera deliciosa*).
(OPPOSITE TOP RIGHT) Bird of paradise (*Strelitzia nicolai*).
(OPPOSITE BOTTOM) Fruit salad plant (*Monstera deliciosa*).
(ABOVE) Devil's ivy (*Epipremnum aureum*).

STYLING TIP
In retail spaces, the aim is to sell more product. Customers often find a sea of products daunting, so introducing the odd plant can better highlight your range.

Plant People

Rena Noordermeer and Samuël Dirksz

Studio Hear Hear

Norway

OCCUPATION: CERAMICIST & PRODUCT MANAGER / WOODTURNER

HTTP://WWW.STUDIOHEARHEAR.COM/ @STUDIOHEARHEAR
@THEENDEAVORIST

HOW MANY PLANTS ARE IN YOUR COLLECTION?
    Around 30.

YOU HAVE A SKILL FOR CREATING TRANQUIL SPACES THAT INCORPORATE A BALANCE OF INTERIORS AND NATURE. HOW AND WHY DO YOU LIKE USING PLANTS IN THE SPACES YOU CREATE?

    Plants just make me happy. To me, an interior without plants feels like an interior without a soul. Minimal homes with calm vibes and clean lines in white, beige and grey are very popular at the moment. Those interiors are stunning, but there's just something missing (plants, it's plants!). They add texture and warmth to a space. You don't have to go full jungle to experience the benefits of green in your interior. If you're looking for a simple eye-catcher, a gorgeous, tall bird of paradise (*Strelitzia nicolai*) or rubber tree (*Ficus elastica*) will definitely do the trick.

YOU MOVED TO NORWAY FROM AMSTERDAM TO BE CLOSER TO NATURE. WHY DO YOU THINK YOU WERE DRAWN TO THIS MOVE?

    We had to move out of our home in Amsterdam a few years ago, and we ended up in a bright loft outside the city. Moving away from Amsterdam made us realise how much stress city life had caused us over the years. The fresh air and slower pace made us feel so much more at ease. With this knowledge, it was easier to expand our views on where to go next. Since Sam is half Norwegian, moving to Norway had always been a subject of conversation. Then Sam got offered a job and we found the farmhouse of my dreams, with gorgeous views and our own forest, so we just decided to go for it.

HOW HAVE YOUR PLANTS RESPONDED TO THE MOVE?

    We had over a hundred plants before the move, but it just wasn't possible to take them all with us. We found new homes for most of them. When it comes to plants, you need to think about a few things: does it get full sun, filtered sun or shade? How much room is there for a plant to grow? How much maintenance

plants. Non-plant people will probably laugh about it, but I get really enthusiastic about plants. The way they grow, the colours, the textures, how they respond to light, etc. Nature never ceases to amaze me!

AS A COUPLE WHO WORKS TOGETHER, HOW HAVE YOU FOUND THE IMPACT OF PLANTS ON YOUR PERSONAL AND WORKING RELATIONSHIP?

Our personal and working relationship feels like one and the same thing. We both draw most of our inspiration from nature and really enjoy a walk outside or a visit to a greenhouse and garden centre. It's great to share this fascination. I might love Sam just a little bit more when he's all excited about some mosses he spotted during a walk in the forest.

IF YOU COULD IMAGINE THE PERFECT CITY, WHAT WOULD IT LOOK LIKE?

My perfect city would definitely look like an urban jungle with a focus on slow living. A place where architecture and nature go hand in hand. A city with lots of parks and places where insects, birds and other animals can thrive. A place that's not all about efficiency and a fast-growing economy, but about balance, sustainability and respect.

does it need? The studio in the Netherlands was a bright loft with high ceilings. The house in Norway is less bright, has smaller rooms and the winter days are darker. So we selected the plants that were suitable for those conditions. Loading them into the moving truck made me very anxious, but they all survived the three-day journey. A few plants dropped some leaves during the winter months, but I'm glad to say they've all pulled through!

DO YOU ALWAYS USE PLANTS WHEN YOU'RE STYLING?

Yes! I can't imagine doing any styling without plants.

FROM AFAR, YOUR PLANTING LOOKS SO EFFORTLESS. HAS GARDENING ALWAYS BEEN EASY FOR YOU?

Taking care of houseplants comes easy to me. I learned a lot about plants during my time at Wildernis, a plant shop in Amsterdam, but I'm also lucky to have 'green fingers'. Gardening, on the other hand, is a completely different story. It's something you can't just do on intuition – you have to have a certain amount of knowledge. I guess I'll learn by trial and error.

HOW WOULD YOU DESCRIBE THE FEELING YOU EXPERIENCE WHEN YOU SEE PLANTS?

It's a feeling of happiness and amazement. I'm totally in my element when we're surrounded by

Chapter 4

Plant care

When it comes to taking care of your plants and garden, it isn't always straightforward. It helps when you can get some foolproof tips from the people around you, including friends, family and your neighbours. Gardening is all about building your knowledge bank and coming to terms with the fact that gardening, like cooking, is going to be personal. What works for others might not work for you, but they will guide you in the right direction.

Nurturing and maintaining my plants and garden is predominantly therapeutic and calming. The only time I find it stressful is when my week is interrupted and I have to be away from home for an extended period of time. That is when I go into 'casualty prevention' mode, accounting for my time away and how much water I'll need to give my garden babies before I go so I don't come home to struggling plants. Plant care shouldn't be overcomplicated, and if you approach it systematically it can be a walk in the park. Always go back to the fundamentals – water, light and nutrition – while taking notice of what works for you, cultivating a list of tricks that motivate your plants to thrive or grow under difficult circumstances.

Everyday gardening

With such a wide array of plants on offer, it can be daunting to figure out what to do to take care of them. When you are feeling overwhelmed, try to remember that gardening has a centuries-long history; you're not expected to soak it all in within a few weeks. It will take time, and even when you think you know what you're doing, nature will throw you a curveball.

No matter how big or small, the key to a well-rounded garden is to be a constant gardener. If you only care for it sporadically, you'll find yourself chasing your tail. The more time you spend caring for your plants, the more you'll learn through practice and patience.

The following pages offer simple, everyday methods I picked up in my early days of gardening – ones I still use today. I hope they help bolster your confidence when tending to your garden.

Tending to your plants should be a therapeutic process. Over time, you'll build up your skill set, and gardening will become second nature. Find ways to garden easily, but also challenge yourself with a range of plant types.

Sowing seeds

Growing plants from seeds is an easy way to expand your plant community without having to spend a lot of money. An immense number of plants can be grown from seed, from edibles to succulents: the list is almost endless. Make sure to refer to the packaging to determine the right time to sow your seeds to ensure they germinate.

YOU WILL NEED

Gloves (optional)

Small punnet or pot

Seed-raising mix

Dibbler or small bamboo stake

Seeds

STEPS

1   Fill a small punnet or pot with nutrient-rich seed-raising mix. Make sure to gently press the soil down with your fingers and repeat until the soil level is 1 cm (½ in) from the top of the pot.

2   Using a dibbler or bamboo stake, create a shallow trough in the soil.

3   Gently scatter your seeds along the trough so they are evenly spaced.

4   Backfill the trough with a thin layer of potting mix and water the soil gently but thoroughly, until the top layer is evenly moist. Put it in a bright spot like a windowsill, but sheltered from harsh direct sunlight.

1

2

3

4

1

2

3

4

5

6

Propagating plant cuttings

One of my favourite ways to propagate plants is by taking cuttings from existing ones. It's also a great way of sharing your plant species with friends and family. Try propagating succulents, cacti and tropical plants to fill your garden.

YOU WILL NEED

Gloves (optional)

Secateurs

Plastic pot or decorative planter

Potting medium

Dibbler or small bamboo stake

Rooting aid/hormone (optional)

STEPS

1 Select a mother plant for propagating. You'll need to choose one that is healthy and lush to ensure the new plants are off to a good start.

2 Using your secateurs, harvest some stem cuttings from the mother plant. Make sure it's a straight cut below the node or branch; ideally your cuttings should be 5–10 cm (2–4 in) long.

3 Fill the pot(s) with potting medium (a premium-grade potting or seed-raising mix will work; however, make sure to use the right potting medium for the plant species you are propagating). You can plant your cuttings in plastic pots or directly into decorative planters. Make sure to gently press the soil down with your fingers and repeat until the soil level is 1 cm (½ in) from the top of the pot.

4 Use a dibbler or stake to make holes in the potting medium for your cuttings. Try to make the holes approximately a third of the length of the chosen cutting.

5 Dip the bottom of the cutting in rooting hormone (if using), then put them into the holes you just made. Use your fingers to press down the potting medium around your cutting to fill any air gaps.

6 Water the soil thoroughly, until the top layer is evenly moist, then put it in a bright spot like a windowsill, but sheltered from harsh direct sunlight. Ensure the soil remains moist at all times.

Pruning and shaping

Pruning and shaping your plants can be daunting, but it really helps promote new, dense growth. When to prune and shape will depend on what type of plant you are pruning, but a good rule of thumb is to prune just before the growing season.

YOU WILL NEED

Secateurs

STEPS

1 Select a plant that needs shaping. Often plants will grow to one side or lack fullness.

2 Begin trimming your plant back to the height you prefer, using this height as your mental guide as you continue on. The best place to prune the stem of a plant is typically above a node or leaf. Try to always prune branches diagonally.

3 Gradually prune branches over the entire plant. Make sure to stand back every now and then, using your eye to judge the shape as you prune.

4 Prune your plant a little tighter if you want to promote compact growth.

1

2

3

4

Training your plants

Young plants often need guidance if you want them to grow a certain way, particularly if they're creeping plants that grow up trees in the wild. Introducing a trellis will allow your plants to attach to a vertical surface, and wire will help direct them to form the shape you prefer.

YOU WILL NEED

Stake, trellis or arch

Twine or wire

Secateurs

STEPS

1 Select a plant that needs training.

2 Place a stake, trellis or arch to the rear of the planter.

3 Secure the branches onto the trellis with twine or wire.

4 Prune off any stray branches to promote denser growth and a fuller plant.

Deadheading

When the blooms on flowering plants start to fade or die, it's time to deadhead them to promote additional flowering and new growth. With edible herbs like basil, you might just want to pinch off their tips with your fingernails to keep them from flowering and going to seed. Pinching also promotes branching and helps control height.

YOU WILL NEED

Secateurs

STEPS

1 Select a plant that needs deadheading.

2 Prune old flowers back to healthy growth, which is usually just below the flower stem.

3 Make sure to prune spent flowers over the whole plant.

4 Continue removing spent flowers, leaving only ones that are still fresh.

1

2

3

4

1

2

3

4

5

6

Repotting

To allow your plants to grow happily, it is good practice to repot them every year or two. You'll know your plants are ready to repot when you see roots growing out of the pot's drainage hole or if the soil is firm when you press the side of the planter. When repotting into a larger planter, try to allow up to 15 cm (6 in) between the root ball and the edge of the pot.

YOU WILL NEED

Gloves (optional)

Skewer or butterknife

Gardening fork

Secateurs

Replacement pot

Trowel

Potting medium

Slow-release fertiliser or organic nutrients as required for your specific plant type

STEPS

1 Loosen the plant's root system in its existing pot. If it's in a plastic pot, gently squeeze the sides to loosen the soil. If it's in a rigid planter, run a butterknife or skewer around the inside of the rim.

2 Remove the plant by positioning your fingers around its trunk and over the soil. Flip the pot upside down, easing the plant out. You may need to gently tap the pot to loosen it.

3 Loosen the root system with a gardening fork or use your fingers.

4 Trim approximately 2 cm (¾ in) off the root ball. This will help promote fresh roots and doesn't hurt the plant.

5 Place a layer of potting medium in your new pot along with a dose of slow-release fertiliser. Place your plant on the bed of soil so that the top of the root ball is approximately 1–2 cm (½–¾ in) below the rim of the pot.

6 Backfill with potting mix and fertilise with slow-release fertiliser as per the package instructions and water in your plant immediately.

Trimming the root ball

When you have a plant and pot combination you adore, you don't always need to repot your plant. Just trim a portion of the root ball and repot it in the same vessel. Pruning the root ball allows for more room to grow, but it also promotes new, healthy root growth to take in lots of nutrients.

YOU WILL NEED

Gloves (optional)

Skewer or butterknife

Gardening fork

Secateurs

Trowel

Potting medium

Slow-release fertiliser or organic nutrients required for your specific plant type

STEPS

1 Loosen the plant's root system in its existing pot. If it's in a plastic pot, gently squeeze the sides to loosen the soil. If it's in a rigid planter, run a butterknife or skewer around the inside of the rim.

2 Remove the plant by positioning your fingers around its trunk and over the soil. Flip the pot upside down, easing the plant out. You may need to gently tap the pot to loosen it.

3 Loosen the roots with a gardening fork or your hands, gently raking off 1 cm (½ in) at a time so you don't shock the plant. Only loosen up to a third of the root ball.

4 Working from the bottom of the root ball, prune up to a third of the root system away.

5 Put a layer of potting medium into your pot along with some slow-release fertiliser as per the package instructions. Place your plant on the soil bed so that the top of the root ball is approximately 1–2 cm (½–¾ in) below the rim of the pot.

6 Backfill with potting mix and fertilise with slow-release fertiliser as per the package instructions and water in your plant immediately.

1

2

3

4

5

6

1

2

3

4

5

6

Group planting

Low planters cry out for a potted landscape that incorporates a range of plants in the one pot, and they make for a great tabletop feature. Make sure to go for two to three plants that require the same light and care, and try combining plants with different textures, forms and heights.

YOU WILL NEED

20 cm (8 in) planter

Trowel

Potting medium

Slow-release fertiliser or organic nutrients required for your specific plant type

Skewer or butterknife

Secateurs

Top dressing as required (pebbles or mulch as preferred)

STEPS

1 Choose your planter and arrange your plants and materials around it.

2 Place a layer of potting mix in the planter along with a dose of slow-release fertiliser as per the package instructions.

3 Loosen one of your plants' root systems in its existing pot. If it's in a plastic pot, gently squeeze the sides to loosen the soil. If it's in a rigid planter, run a butterknife or skewer around the inside of the rim. Remove the plant by positioning your fingers around its trunk and over the soil. Flip the pot upside down, easing the plant out. You may need to gently tap the pot to loosen it. If the root ball is too big for the planter, you can trim the roots back (page 150). Just make sure to only trim up to a third of the root ball.

4 Arrange the plant in the new planter as you like, thinking about where you'll place the other two. You want to allow space for your plants to grow, so plant them approximately 2–3 cm (¾–1¼ in) from one another.

5 Repeat steps 2–4 with the rest of your plants. Make sure to place them on the bed of soil so that the top of the root ball is approximately 1–2 cm (½–¾ in) below the rim of the pot.

6 Backfill with potting mix and fertilise with slow-release fertiliser as per the package instructions. Finish with top dressing as required and water in your plants immediately.

Additional propagation techniques

Air layering

Air layering is a propagation technique that creates new plants from stems or branches still attached to the mother plant. Root growth is encouraged by wrapping sphagnum moss or soil around the chosen branch, a process that occurs naturally in the wild when branches touch the ground and root. At home, it's a simple and economical way to propagate more established plants.

PLANT TYPES

Woody plants such as citrus, fruit trees, *Ficus*.

WHAT YOU NEED

Knife
Brush
Rooting aid/hormone
*Recycled plastic bag, handles and
    bottom removed*
Twine or wire
Damp sphagnum moss
Secateurs

STEPS

1 Select a healthy branch that is straight and easily accessible. Aim to propagate one that is 30–100 cm (1 ft–3 ft 3 in) long. The branch should be between 1–3 cm (½–1¼ in) thick.

2 With a sharp knife, peel back 2–3 cm (¾–1¼ in) of bark where you want the new roots to grow.

3 Brush some rooting hormone around the exposed branch where the bark has been removed.

4 With twine or wire, tie the plastic bag 3 cm (1¼ in) below the exposed portion of the branch. You may need to remove any leaves that are below the exposed branch.

5 Fill the bag with moist sphagnum moss, evenly distributing it around the branch. Keep filling until the exposed branch is concealed, but leave enough room at the top so the bag can be tied.

6 Close the top of the plastic bag with wire or twine.

7 Over the next few months, monitor the moss to ensure it stays moist but isn't saturated. If it dries out, carefully open the top and water. You'll know the air-layered plant is ready to be cut when you see a healthy root system emerging.

8 Cut the stem below the bottom tie, remove the plastic and pot up the propagated plant.

Layering

Layering is an easy way to propagate houseplants and outdoor cuttings while they're still attached to the mother plant, allowing them to stay happily fed before being released to fend for themselves.

PLANT TYPES

Climbing and trailing plants.

WHAT YOU NEED

Small pot

Potting medium

Bobby pin or wire

Secateurs

STEPS

1 Select a healthy branch. It helps to choose one close to the bottom of the plant and one that is easily pliable.

2 Fill a small pot with potting medium.

3 Place the pot near the mother plant where it can sit happily for a while without being disturbed. Without cutting or breaking the chosen branch, guide it over the potting medium and secure it with a bobby pin or by bending some wire into a U shape. You may need to remove some foliage where it touches the soil.

4 Keep the soil moist, but not drenched. You'll know your plant has rooted when you notice new growth. The stem can then be cut to release it from the mother plant. Now that your new plant is on its own, keep it in its current pot until it's big enough to be repotted. Put your plant in a place that has conditions it likes.

Grafting

Grafting is a technique practised by horticulturalists and gardeners where a cutting of one plant is joined to the base of another plant to allow the two to grow as one. This technique allows plants to grow stronger and encourages them to become disease resistant.

PLANT TYPES

Citrus, fruit trees, woody plants, cacti.

WHAT YOU NEED

Sharp knife

Secateurs

Grafting tape

STEPS

1 Make sure to graft at the right time of year for your chosen plant. The rootstock (the host plant, which is a stem with a well-developed root system) should be a similar thickness to the scion (the top part of the plant, which will be attached to the rootstock) taken from the mother plant.

2 Make a 3–6 cm (1¼–2½ in) angled or V cut on the rootstock.

3 Choose a scion and trim it from the mother plant. It should be approximately 10–15 cm (4–6 in) long, or the length of 2–3 buds, all leaves removed.

4 Prepare the scion by making a 3–6 cm (1¼–2½ in) angled or V cut just like the host stock, but in the opposite direction.

5 Fit the host and scion together so that their cambiums (growth tissues) line up.

6 Using the grafting tape, secure the joint by wrapping it around tightly to seal the cuts. Over the next few months, the joint will naturally fuse together.

Tips and tricks for making sure your plants thrive

IRRIGATION

To take some of the pressure off, consider installing an irrigation system to water your outdoor plants. It's the perfect way to keep your plants hydrated, particularly if you have a busy schedule.

HARNESSING SHADE

Some plants require more shade than others. For those that don't like much sun, make sure to position them under a sheltering tree or structure. Look around to see how the sun moves through your space before deciding which spot will be best.

CREATING SHELTER

Spaces exposed to the elements, like extreme wind and sun, may need a helping hand to make them habitable. Use materials such as a shade cloth to provide shelter for plants. It also helps to cluster them together so that the hardier plants provide shelter for more delicate ones.

LAYERING

Creating a layered indoor or outdoor garden can help your plants thrive as it increases the humidity in the air surrounding the plant clusters. If planting groups of plants, ensure that specimen plants (the focal point of your planting) and companion plants do not compete for light and nutrients. When choosing plants for your space, take note of their height and form.

PLANTS IN SMALL SPACES

Most urban indoor spaces are likely smaller than we'd like, but that shouldn't preclude you from filling them with plants. Styling with plant stands and hanging planters can help raise a plant to the right height and let it breathe, visually speaking, by separating it from other elements in your space. By raising your plant off the floor, letting it cascade from a ceiling beam, or draping it around shelves, you can also harness the best light conditions in your space to ensure that your plants are happy. This principle also works well for outdoor spaces such as verandas and balconies.

Home composting

Composting at home is a great way to minimise waste and put your discarded produce to good use, and it doesn't have to be difficult. There are plenty of gadgets on the market that make traditional composting in small spaces achievable and practical.

Worm farms make great composting units, allowing you to recycle your food scraps and turn them into both solid and liquid fertilisers. There are also compact composting bins, which makes composting in apartments much easier.

Like anything in life, balance is important when it comes to using compost on plants. Make sure not to overuse your compost: you're shooting for approximately one part compost to two parts potting medium. Ensure the compost is cool and is mixed in evenly.

YOU WILL NEED

Small compost unit. I recommend a worm farm, urban composter or Bokashi bin.

A range of organic waste such as fruit, vegetables, egg shells, coffee grinds, dry leaves, plant cuttings and tea leaves

Potting medium

Newspaper or cardboard (shredded is best)

HOW TO COMPOST

It's important to ensure your compost is healthy. For a well-balanced compost mix, aim to have one part green material (plant matter and food scraps) to four parts brown material (cardboard, straw, dry leaves).

Place about 5 cm (2 in) of potting mix in the bottom of your compost bin. Add a layer of newspaper on top.

Add some organic material, either food- or plant-based, into your compost bin.

Make sure to stir and aerate your compost once a week. This allows air and heat to move through it, and provides oxygen to any active microbes. If your compost seems to dry, add some water to moisten it, but ensure it does not become soggy.

HOW TO USE COMPOST IN YOUR GARDEN OR POTS

When your compost has completely decomposed, it's time to use it for your plants. You will know your compost is ready to use when it looks like dark soil.

Sprinkle a handful or two in with each plant, depending on the size of your planter. Refer to the ratios of compost to potting mix above.

Use a trowel to mix your compost into the potting mix around your plant.

Top-layer dressing and mulch

To prevent too much moisture from evaporating from your garden or planters, you might consider adding a top layer of mulch or dressing gravel. Apply a layer of minimum 5 cm (2 in) thickness. It will conserve moisture by creating a blanket of insulation between the soil and the air. There are a range of materials you can use, which will depend on what appeals to you and what is best for your plants.

When it comes to potted plants outdoors, I prefer to use a bark-based mulch. For arid species, I often use a fine gravel that simulates their natural environment. The chosen dressing should reflect the aesthetic of the space; there is nothing worse than a dressing that seems at odds with its surroundings.

For indoor plants, I don't apply mulch as it restricts everyday care and limits soil aeration.

TYPES OF TOP-LAYER DRESSING

> Gravel
>
> Bark
>
> Sugar cane
>
> Sand
>
> Pebbles

Plant People

Chen Attar
We Love Plants

Tel Aviv, Israel

OCCUPATION: STORE OWNER WE LOVE PLANTS

@WELOVEPLANTSTLV

HOW MANY PLANTS DO YOU HAVE?

Over 100.

WHAT INSPIRED YOU TO OPEN YOUR STORE?

After a long period of feeling unfulfilled and unsatisfied, I left a job as a content manager, took a long vacation and some time to find out what I wanted to do. All my life I have envied people who can turn huge love and inspiration into a profession. The search lasted for several months, and at the end of it I realized that I wanted to work with plants. I realized that I had grown up in an environment surrounded by plants, and found that this is where I find peace, tranquility and security. As a child I used to run away to the garden in my parents' house, tended the plants, looked at them, studied them, lay on the grass for hours to see and hear the sound of insects. I realized that I wanted to be surrounded by plants, to care for them, and to pass this quiet joy to others. In 2016, I opened my first store in Tel Aviv with huge help from my partner, Michal, who designed the space and generally provided tremendous inspiration and a safety net for my dream to come true.

WHAT TYPES OF PLANTS DO YOU FIND THE MOST SUCCESSFUL IN YOUR CLIMATE?

Tel Aviv is a hot and humid city in the summer, while in winter it is cool and sometimes rainy. The climate is very suitable for cacti and tropical plants such as *Monstera*, *Philodendron*, and *Ficus* of various types. These plants are very easy to treat and loved by many Tel Avivians.

WHERE DO YOU DRAW INSPIRATION FROM WHEN CHOOSING PLANTS AND PRODUCTS FOR YOUR STORE?

I draw inspiration from my partner in life, Michal. She is a ceramic artist and a multidisciplinary designer, an artist in her soul, and has a brilliant brain for detail and design. Whenever I choose a plant or a planter I ask myself, 'Would Michal like it?' Then I try to figure out whether the plant is suitable for my clientele, what planter it can fit, whether it's interesting and current, whether it's exciting. I choose plants with my gut and emotion, with some modest help from my head. A perfect pairing is always what I'm looking for.

WHAT IS THE PLANT COMMUNITY LIKE IN TEL AVIV?

The Tel Aviv plant community is still in its very early stages. In Israel in general, there is very little gardening and plant culture. Although plants have always been part of the urban landscape and within our houses, there is no deep culture around plants. But there has been a revival, with the rapid pace of urban living. People who understand design are starting to want to

DO YOU BELIEVE EVERYONE HAS THE ABILITY TO GARDEN?

I don't believe that everyone has a natural tendency to gardening. It's a relationship – it's love. The secret to getting better at it lies in listening and paying attention, which you can learn over the years. Plants that die break the heart, but they can also help you learn from the mistakes of the past.

DESCRIBE THE RELATIONSHIP BETWEEN PLANTS AND PLANTERS.

There is a deep connection between house plants and the planters in which they live. I believe that every plant has a suitable planter, an appropriate pairing that strengthens the plant and makes it look more impressive. In the shop, I try to bring a collection of planters that tell a story and complement the urban environment. I am very fond of handmade planters, and Michal opened a ceramic studio under the PLUSOPLUS brand that explores the relationship between plants and planters. She is one of the pioneers in Tel Aviv in understanding the connection between plants and planters, and creating ones that feel luxurious, fashionable, up-to-date and very special.

bring the outside in. At the same time, the market in Israel is relatively small and most plants are imported from countries like Holland and England. In the store I meet a lot of young people who love plants, but want to grow their own.

WHAT ARE YOUR THOUGHTS ON PLANTS IN OUR URBAN SURROUNDINGS AND HOW OUR CITIES CAN BE SHAPED AROUND GREENERY?

We tend to think of plants in our urban environments as green lungs, helping to balance the effects of industrialization and environmental pollution. But they have other important functions: they form breeding habitats for insects and birds, prevent soil erosion and even balance high winds. Plants soothe us as we rest in the shade of the trees and play with children on the lawn. They provide us with refuge and an island of sanity. Adding as many plants as possible to city centers will strengthen and intensify the effects they have on us. They affect us in a way that we cannot always put our finger on, but we can always feel their positive influence.

FOR THOSE WANTING PLANTS FOR A HARSH ENVIRONMENT, WHAT ARE YOUR TIPS?

I have a recommendation that will fit any environment: develop a relationship with your plants. I believe that plants communicate their feelings and tell us when to take care of them. They reveal when they are thirsty, when they are sad or happy. Plants almost always broadcast exactly what they need; we just have to look carefully.

Chapter 5

What to do in an emergency

Gardening doesn't always go to plan, and sometimes plants struggle. Don't panic! Your plants will find ways of signalling when they aren't happy, and all you have to do is pay attention and stay calm. Keep track of how your plant looked when you first bought it, then take note of any changes in foliage and growth over time. Pay attention to the mood of your plants and how they respond to changes in weather, light and air quality.

Regular plant maintenance and care is the key to keeping your plants healthy. At the start of spring and autumn, make sure to clean your foliage by hosing plants down in the shower, or outside if you have the space. Be careful not to expose your indoor plants to extreme weather conditions when doing this and bring them back in as soon as possible. If your plants are too large to move or it's easier to clean them where they are, use a cloth and a bucket of water combined with a few drops of detergent to gently wipe down the leaves. Remember to clean both the top and bottom to minimise the risk of disease and pests.

The trick with plant problems is to shortlist what may be wrong and address these problems one by one until your plant is happy again. Start by checking in on the fundamentals: water, light and nutrition. Is your plant getting enough sun? Has it been overwatered? Does it need a fertiliser boost? If your plants are plagued by pests and disease, try to pinpoint what kind of pest or disease is affecting your plant. Pay attention to particular symptoms, which will guide you to the best solution.

If that doesn't help, it may be time to try and save what you can. This might involve drastic measures like heavy pruning, but take heart: plants are stronger than we think they are. If they can survive a natural disaster, then they might just survive a domestic one.

Tips and tricks for difficult environments

LOW-LIT SPACES

From the outset, try choosing plants that require less natural light. My trick in low-lit spaces is to occasionally move my plants into a space with more natural light for a little while. Choose hardy plants, then swap them in and out of a well-lit space every two weeks or so.

INACCESSIBLE AREAS

In less accessible spaces, or if you just don't have the time for frequent watering, choose plants that are well suited to drier conditions. In outdoor spaces, you can install a simple irrigation system to assist with watering during warmer months.

POOR-QUALITY SOIL

Not all homes and garden beds have premium-quality soil. If your soil is rock hard, not absorbing water or holding onto water for too long, it may be a good idea to aerate it (see page 184), improve the drainage, apply some water-absorbing crystals, and mix in additional organic matter and compost to build up its quality (for more on composting, see page 162).

STUFFY ROOMS

Fresh air is important to plants, both indoors and out. Make sure to avoid stagnant air, which can invite pests and diseases. Often, all you have to do is open the windows. Even placing plants in high-traffic areas can provide them with a little air.

HOT SUMMERS

Pay close attention when the weather heats up. When the days become hotter, you will need to water more frequently to make up for moisture evaporating from the soil. You will know it's time to water when the top 2–3 cm (¾–1¼ in) of soil dries out or your plant is drooping; that is a plant's way of letting you know that it's thirsty. Mulching is a great way to preserve moisture in outdoor plants (for more on mulching, see page 165).

GOING AWAY ON HOLIDAY

Going on holiday can be stressful for gardeners, who worry about how their plants will fare while they're away. For small collections of plants, you can buy yourself some time by placing them in trays of water. I don't recommend this for everyday gardening, but for short periods – especially during summer – it can help save your plants from dehydration.

When it comes to large collections and in-ground plants, you'll need to enlist the help of a friend to plant-sit.

RENTALS

Styling your home is an age-old problem for renters. It never quite feels like you can put your own personal mark on the space. That's the beauty of styling with plants: they can quickly convert a rented space into one that feels grounded and comfortable. If you're on a budget, buy small plants and nurture them into larger ones while you save your pennies for your dream home. I recommend sticking to neutral-coloured planters, as there is less risk of them becoming dated as design trends evolve.

Common plant myths

ARTIFICIAL LIGHTING WORKS FOR PLANTS

Don't count on artificial lights to nourish your indoor gardens. Unless you are using UV lights, your typical lightbulb will not help your plants grow. Make sure to choose plants that will thrive in the natural lighting conditions on offer.

MISTING IS THE SAME AS WATERING

Misting your plants can't stand in for a thorough root water. It's important to water your plants' root systems as well as occasionally misting the foliage.

BROWN FOLIAGE REGENERATES

Once foliage goes brown, it's not going to go green again. Remove dead foliage to keep your plant tidy.

BOTTLED WATER IS BETTER

I call this the 'Evian experience'. Bottled water is not better for your plants and is an entirely unnecessary expense. Rainwater is great; however, I don't expect everyone will harvest rainwater for their gardens, and they don't have to. Tap water will do.

SOME PLANTS THRIVE ON NEGLECT

As convenient as this one is to believe, all plants require nurturing. Yes, some plants can last a long while without care, but weekly to fortnightly maintenance is recommended if you want your plants to thrive.

A BIGGER POT MEANS A PLANT WILL GROW FASTER

Definitely not. In fact, putting your plants in a planter that is too big for it can have the opposite effect. It leaves the plant exposed to soil that remains too damp, which often leads to root rot. Potting up gradually is more effective and will help you avoid upsetting your plants.

Plant problems

Plants can suffer from a range of problems, including disease, pests, neglect and even too much attention (read: overwatering and overfertilising). These issues include:

Root rot

Sunburn/frostburn

Physical damage

Pests and diseases

Fertiliser burn

Drastic underwatering

Have a look at frequent seasonal plant problems (and how to treat them) on pages 44–47. Below is a list of the most common diseases that can affect your plant, with treatments for each. Pages 176–177 detail common pests and pages 178–181 list home remedies to combat disease- or pest-borne plant issues.

Common diseases

DISEASE	SYMPTOM	TREATMENT
Anthracnose	Black sunken spots on foliage	Remove and dispose of infected foliage. Spray with natural fungicide and make sure to keep the foliage dry for several weeks.
Bacterial blight	Small, pale green, blister-like spots on leaves that cause wilting	Remove and dispose of infected leaves and treat with natural fungicide. Reduce moisture and avoid misting.
Botrytis blight	Rotting brown leaves and stems with fuzzy grey spores that usually appear in humid weather	Remove and dispose of infected leaves, flowers and stems. Spray with natural fungicide and make sure to keep the foliage dry for several weeks.

DISEASE	SYMPTOM	TREATMENT
Crown or stem rot	Part of crown or stem has gone brown and soft	Remove affected parts of the plant and drench with natural fungicide. Allow soil to dry out before watering.
Damping off	Rot in the root system, causing plants to fall over	Remove affected plants and improve air circulation and drainage. Avoid overwatering.
Leaf spot	Small, circular yellow or brown irregular spots	Remove and dispose of infected foliage. Spray with natural fungicide and ensure good air circulation around your plant.
Powdery mildew	White-to-grey powdery fungal growth that appears on the surface of leaves and sometimes on flower petals	Spray with natural fungicide.
Rust	Round brown spores on the underside of leaves	Remove leaves and dispose of the infected foliage.
Sooty mould	Dusty black, sticky fungus that covers leaves, stems and branches	Wash off the fungus with soap and water. Spray with natural fungicide.

Common pests

MEALY BUG

Small, white, furry insects that feed on foliage. When left untreated for long periods, they cause foliage to turn yellow and die.

Treat Wash leaves and spray them with natural pesticide (page 178–79).

SCALE

Small brown or black bumps attached to leaves and branches. Causes plants to wilt, yellow and slowly die. Scale sometimes excrete sticky residue on leaves and trunks.

Treat Pick off and gently scrub visible scale on leaves and branches. Alternatively, use an insecticide spray such as neem oil (page 178), but be cautious when using it on soft, delicate leaves.

SNAILS AND SLUGS

You'll see these hungry creatures feeding on foliage, leaving a shiny trail in their wake.

Treat Hand-remove them from your plants, making sure to look on the undersides of leaves and under pots and rims. If required, use snail and slug bait, but be careful around children and pets. You can also make a beer trap: fill a small container with beer and place it in your garden bed. Snails and slugs will be drawn to the beer and get trapped there.

THRIP

These tiny black insects jump from plant to plant, leaving silvery smudges. They feed on leaves and buds and distort growth, leaving leaves spotted and stumpy.

Treat Wash leaves and spray them with natural pesticide (page 178–79).

CATERPILLARS

These crawling pests come in a range of colours, burrow through foliage and leave droppings behind.

Treat Hand-remove them from your plants, making sure to look on the undersides of leaves.

EARWIG

A dark-brown insect with a pincer tail; it leaves ragged holes in foliage.

Treat Hand-remove them from your plants, making sure to look on the undersides of leaves. Gently reshape the plant if necessary.

MILLIPEDE

These crawling insects are found in soil or around pots and feed off roots and rhizomes.

Treat Make sure to regularly remove old debris from around your plants and keep the area clean. Wash leaves and spray them with natural pesticide (page 178–79).

BIRDS

Birds can wreak havoc in gardens, digging up the soil around plants, breaking branches and eating produce. But they can be a wonderful addition to your green oasis too.

Treat Net any edibles, ensuring there are no openings.

FUNGUS GNAT

Tiny black flying insects that thrive in constantly wet soil.

Treat To treat adult gnats, use sticky yellow insect traps (from your local supermarket, nursery or hardware store). To treat eggs in the soil, remove any decaying plant matter from the pot, then remove the top 2–5 cm (¾–2 in) of soil and discard it. Let the remaining soil dry out, then drench it with neem oil pesticide (page 178). Treat multiple times five days apart.

WHITE FLY

A small white fly that causes leaves to turn yellow and drop.

Treat Spray with natural pesticide (page 178–79). Treat multiple times until the flies aren't present anymore. Make sure treatments are five days apart.

SPIDER MITE

These sap-sucking insects appear as reddish-brown specks. They feed off leaves, eventually turning them yellow.

Treat Dilute a few teaspoons of detergent in water and use it to clean the leaves by wiping, then treat them with neem oil pesticide (page 178). Repeat every five days until the mites are gone.

POSSUMS

Possums can make gardeners tear their hair out. They devour foliage, often leading to the plant's death.

Treat There are many preventative measures and treatments, such as spraying foliage with garlic (page 179), chilli (page 178) and store-bought possum deterrent. There are also electronic devices designed to emit ultrasonic blasts that fend off hungry possums. The success of these methods tends to be short-lived, so you may need to net vulnerable plants.

APHIDS

Small green insects that suck the juices out of plants.

Treat Use a mild soap mixture or a natural pesticide (page 178–79).

Natural remedies for pests and diseases

I grew up using chemicals to motivate my garden to grow faster, provide a bigger harvest or look a certain way. Now I prefer to use natural methods. Before humans had ready access to chemicals, there was a whole array of natural homemade solutions to treat plant pests and diseases. Natural remedies can be simple to make, and require little more than ingredients you probably have at home already.

Becoming better acquainted with the horticultural industry over the past few years has taught me that every industry and individual can become more conscious of how what we do and use affects our environment. It's the little things we do every day that can have the biggest impact on our plants and community.

Neem oil pesticide

Works well as a general-purpose insecticide for spraying on soil and foliage.

YOU WILL NEED

1 litre (34 fl oz/4 cups) water

1–2 tsp liquid soap or dishwashing detergent

2 tsp neem oil

spray bottle or mister

METHOD

1 Mix the water, detergent and neem oil directly in your spray bottle or mister.

2 Spray directly onto pest-affected plants, ensuring insects and foliage are adequately covered. Apply on a sunny day, avoiding evening or early morning.

3 Continue the treatment every 5–7 days until all traces of pests are removed.

Chilli pesticide

Great for treating pests such as aphids, whitefly and mealy bugs.

YOU WILL NEED

½ cup fresh chilli or chilli powder

500 ml (17 fl oz/2 cups) water

1 tsp liquid soap or dishwashing detergent

spray bottle or mister

METHOD

1 In a blender, combine the chilli and 1 cup water and pulse until they form a paste.

2 In a saucepan, bring the chilli paste and the remaining 1 cup water to a boil.

3 Strain the mixture into a spray bottle along with the liquid soap.

4 Spray directly onto pest-affected plants, ensuring insects and foliage are adequately covered. Continue the treatment every 5–7 days until all traces of pests are removed.

Garlic pesticide

Perfect for treating pests such as aphids, whitefly and mealy bugs.

YOU WILL NEED

2 bulbs garlic

1 litre (34 fl oz/4 cups) water

spray bottle or mister

CONCENTRATE

½ tsp vegetable oil

1 tsp liquid soap or dishwashing detergent

750 ml (25½ fl oz/3 cups) water

METHOD

1　Combine the garlic and 60 ml (2 fl oz/¼ cup) of water in a blender and pulse until it forms a paste.

2　Let the mixture sit in a jar or bowl overnight.

3　To make the concentrate, strain the mixture into a clean jar, then add the vegetable oil and liquid soap. Fill the jar with the water and mix.

4　To make the spray, combine 1 cup of the concentrate with 1 litre (34 fl oz/4 cups) water in a spray bottle and mix well.

5　Spray directly onto pest-affected plants, ensuring insects and foliage are adequately covered. Continue the treatment every 5–7 days until all traces of pests are removed.

Ginger pesticide

Perfect for treating pests such as mealy bugs.

YOU WILL NEED

¾ cup of finely chopped ginger

1 litre (34 fl oz/4 cups) water

1 tsp liquid soap or dishwashing detergent

spray bottle or mister

METHOD

1 In a saucepan, bring the ginger and water to a boil.

2 Strain the mixture into a spray bottle along with the liquid soap.

3 Spray directly onto pest-affected plants, ensuring insects and foliage are adequately covered. Continue the treatment every 5–7 days until all traces of pests are removed.

Natural fungicide

Great for treating a range of pests and diseases: mould, powdery mildew, root rot, spider mites, mealy bugs and more.

YOU WILL NEED

1.15 litres (39 fl oz/4½ cups) water

1 drop vegetable or neem oil

1 drop liquid soap or dishwashing detergent

2 tsp bicarbonate of soda (baking soda)

spray bottle or mister

METHOD

1   In your spray bottle or mister, mix the water, oil, detergent and bicarbonate of soda.

2   Spray directly onto the infected plant, ensuring all infected areas are covered in the solution. Apply on a hot, sunny day, avoiding evenings and early mornings. Continue the treatment every 5–7 days until all fungal traces are removed.

Epsom salt tonic

Perfect for nutrient-deficient plants, promoting lush growth and flowers, and deterring pests.

YOU WILL NEED

Epsom salt (½ tbsp for spray solution; 1 tbsp for direct application)

as much water as needed to fill your spray bottle

spray bottle or mister

FOR SPRAY SOLUTION

1   Pour ½ tbsp salt into a spray bottle, then fill the rest up with water.

2   Shake well until the salt particles dissolve. Spray directly onto foliage every 2 weeks.

FOR DIRECT APPLICATION

1   Wet your plant's soil.

2   Sprinkle 1 tbsp Epsom salt onto the soil every 3–4 weeks.

Plant People

Katie Marx

Butterland

Newstead, Australia

OCCUPATION: FLORIST

HTTP://WWW.BUTTERLAND.COM.AU/
@KATIEMARXFLOWERS

HOW MANY PLANTS DO YOU HAVE?

Around 30.

TELL US ABOUT YOUR DAILY ROUTINE AND HOW
PLANTS ARE INVOLVED.

What routine?! No day is the same – we live a
varied and diverse life involving children and school
activities, floral work in the city and country, events
and weddings, foraging and harvesting.

Our house is always full of plants in various forms.
The branches of wild fruit, maybe, seasonal flowers,
blossom or moss, fungi and interesting things the
children have found. Our whole family is interested
in nature, and we all notice and appreciate the way
plants change with the seasons.

WHAT LED YOU TO BECOME A FLORIST?

My mum told me I couldn't live in a Kombi van for
the rest of my life and that I had to do something I
loved. It was also Mum who suggested a career
involving flowers would suit me. I had visions of
formal arrangements wrapped in plastic and wasn't
keen. Luckily I gave floristry a go, and my first success
was winning a competition for arranging flowers in a
gumboot! This was in New Zealand, where I grew up:
a lot of gumboots there.

I came to Australia, working in Sydney and
Melbourne, followed by a stint in London. My passion
for flowers and design only increased and I have never
regretted becoming a florist.

YOUR INSTALLATIONS ALWAYS LOOK PHENOMENAL
AND EMOTIONAL. HOW HAS THE RELATIONSHIP
BETWEEN LIVE PLANT AND CUT FLOWER EVOLVED
DURING YOUR CAREER?

As I grew my business, I was able to experiment with
unusual materials, larger installations, plant material
that was not considered pretty or predictable, and to
develop a style that became more about what I love.
Fortunately other people seem to like it too.

My relationship with both live plants and cut
flowers is about bringing them all together in a way
that feels natural and evocative of their place in the
natural world.

WHAT INSPIRED YOU TO INVEST SO MUCH LOVE
INTO BUTTERLAND?

Butterland is both our home and our passion. We
are lucky to be custodians of such a beautiful old
building, and have always worked to blend the history
and stories of Butterland into the hopefully sensitive
renovation.

We enjoy helping other people hold events at
Butterland that are special to them, and love that it
is woven into their stories as well. We believe this
beautiful place deserves all the love bestowed upon it.

YOU HAVE AN EXTENSIVE INDOOR AND OUTDOOR
GARDEN. HOW DO YOU MANAGE MAINTENANCE AND
WHAT ARE YOUR TIPS?

Our bathroom, which was the old butter factory
laboratory, is the best place ever for lots of my
favourite indoor plants. Showers are reminiscent of a
tropical rainforest downpour. Talk to your plants, but
don't overwater: that's my best tip.

My outdoor garden at the front is full of textural
plants. My favourite is the smoke bush (Cotinus
coggygria), which has featured in several stunning
wedding photos. I keep maintenance to a minimum

using mulch and mass plantings, letting things go through their seasonal changes without interfering too much.

WE ALWAYS SEE YOU FORAGING WITH YOUR FAMILY, BUT ALSO WITH CLOSE FRIENDS IN THE INDUSTRY. HOW DID THIS COME ABOUT AND HOW HAS THIS COMMUNITY SHAPED YOUR THOUGHTS ON TURNING NATURE INTO INSTALLATION?

I grew up in rural New Zealand among a large country garden with lots of deciduous, orchard and native trees, as well as a creek and bush to play in, so my childhood meant I developed a great love and appreciation of nature from an early age. I remember coming home with armfuls of large, mossy branches, drilling holes in my bedroom ceiling for hooks to hang them up, and sleeping among what felt like an enchanted forest. My parents left it there for ages, even after I left home. I also remember picking every one of my nana's precious and long-awaited daffodils when I was about four years old.

I have loved picking and arranging natural materials all my life, while always appreciating that Mother Nature is the best installation artist of all.

YOUR WORK AND GARDEN OOZE PERSONALITY. WHAT ARE YOUR TIPS FOR NEW FLORISTS AND GARDENERS WHEN IT COMES TO PUTTING YOUR TOUCH ON YOUR PROJECTS?

Just stay true to yourself and your instincts. Be inspired by others, but let your own style evolve and tell your own story. There are no rules ... well, maybe

a few, but even those can be broken as you develop confidence and feel your abilities develop. Love the plants you choose to work with, respect them and don't be afraid to try something different. Above all, just relax and enjoy the creative process.

Glossary

AERATOR
A tool, such as a dibbler (or even a chopstick), for aerating soil to allow oxygen, water and nutrients to penetrate it.

AIR LAYERING
A propagation technique for propagating new trees or shrubs from branches still attached to the parent plant. The stem is wrapped with moist sphagnum moss or soil to promote root growth.

ARID
An environment with little or no rain.

ARTIFICIAL SEASON
A climatic condition resulting from heating and cooling.

BACKFILLING
Refilling a pot with soil once a plant has been placed into the pot.

CLIMATE
Weather conditions predominant in a place over time.

CULTIVAR
A plant variety produced through selective breeding.

CUTTING
A piece of a plant harvested from an established plant to create a new plant.

DAPPLED LIGHT
Natural light that has been filtered through the leaves of trees or through a window if indoors.

DEADHEADING
The removal of dead and spent flowerheads.

DECIDUOUS
A plant that sheds its leaves annually.

DIBBLER
A pointy hand tool used for planting seeds, seedlings and cuttings.

DORMANCY
A period where the plant slows growth to preserve energy for the growing season.

DRENCH
To soak the soil thoroughly.

DRY GARDEN
A garden specifically curated with drought-tolerant plants.

GERMINATION
Sprouting of seeds after a period of dormancy.

GRAFTING
A propagation technique whereby a plant is transplanted onto a host plant.

HEIRLOOM
An old cultivar of a plant that is passed down over generations.

LAYERING
Curating a collection of plants to create a visually appealing grouping of texture, colour and form.

MICROCLIMATE
A controlled climate that replicates a natural environment on a smaller scale.

MEDITERRANEAN
An environment with hot, dry summers and wet winters.

NATIVE
A plant indigenous to a place.

NEEM OIL
A natural vegetable oil produced from the fruit and seed of the neem tree, used for pest control.

NODE
The part of the plant where the petiole meets the stem of the plant. A node typically holds one or two leaves.

PEAT MOSS
Decomposed sphagnum moss. Used in potting mixes and soils to retain water and nutrients.

PERENNIAL
A plant that lives for several years.

PETIOLE
The stalk that joins the leaf to the stem of the plant.

PROPAGATION
Creating and multiplying plants from parent plants through a range of techniques.

ROOT BALL
The main mass of roots at the base of the plant.

ROOT BOUND
A condition where the plant's root system is confined and the roots become densely tangled within the pot.

ROOTING AID/HORMONE
A product (either artificial or natural) that stimulates root growth in propagated cuttings.

SPHAGNUM MOSS
A natural moss used in gardening for its ability to store large quantities of water.

SUCKER
A shoot growing from the base or root of the plant that becomes a new plant.

TEMPERATE
An environment bearing mild temperatures.

TRAINING
Manually assisting a plant by using plant ties and stakes to direct the plant to grow a certain way.

VARIEGATION
Multi-coloured or patterned leaves or stems.

VENTILATION
A supply of fresh air to a room or space.

Naming conventions

Plant names can be confusing at the best of times. When it comes to naming plants, each plant is identified through a scientific naming convention specific to taxonomy. Plants are identified typically by Latin or Latinised words from other languages, beginning with family, genus and then species.

Consider the genus the generic name and the species name the specific name associated to the plant. Where plants have been hybridised or cultivated by humans, they will have a cultivar name usually assigned at the end of the plant's name. For the everyday, plants can also be identified by common or vernacular names. Common names are usually specific to country and location. Consider common names a plant's nickname.

For example, the widely grown devil's ivy (*Epipremnum aureum*) will have the following naming convention:

COMMON NAME: devil's ivy
FAMILY: Araceae
GENUS: *Epipremnum*
SPECIES: *aureum*

Index

For different plant types in situ, refer to the balcony (pages 79–81), courtyard (pages 85–9), porches, entrances and hallways (pages 91–5) and indoor oasis (pages 99–113) sections.

Thank you

It's fair to say that the last couple of years have been a whirlwind adventure, full of highs but also lows. A journey that has made me realise who I really am and which has highlighted my passion for plants. The support of the plant and design community has been one I will never take for granted.

My family has supported us from day one. When we have needed them for advice, or just to make sure we weren't going insane, they were always there.

To my book partner in crime, Armelle Habib. You always make me smile with how you capture a moment in time. You're an inspiration and it's an honour to have you as a friend.

A big thank you to the amazing team at Hardie Grant, who have worked around the clock to make this book come together. It's as much their book as mine. Anna Collett: I am so thankful we crossed paths. Jane Willson, who allowed me to explore freely. Thanks to Kate Armstrong for challenging each word with a magnifying glass, to Andy Warren for putting my personality on paper, and Shelley Steer for her beautiful illustrations.

The beautiful spaces in this book are thanks to Heather Nette King, Kegan Harry and Lachie Gibson of Angle, Bree Leech, Andy Paltos, Roz and Nicola Matear, Meg and Zenta Tanaka of CIBI, Sally Gordon, Cindy-Lee Davies and 'Willie' of Lightly, Mitchell Jones and Cara Stizza of Studio Studio, Jerry Wolveridge of Wolveridge Architects, Brad Kooyman of Drunken Barber, Trisha Garner and Simon Tan, Carole Whiting, Nick Hughes of Keoma, Rachel Soh and Richard Janko, Armelle Habib, Phoebe Simmonds of Blow Bar, Stuart McKenzie of South of Johnston, Anna Rozen and Taj Darvall, Michael Mabuti and Susan Chung.

To Meg and Zenta Tanaka: where do we even begin? Thank you for receiving us with open arms and making us your family.

To Heather Nette King, who only needs to say one word to get me to believe in myself. Thanks for being such a loving mentor.

To Indira Naidoo, who reached out and gave me comfort as this journey took off. Thanks for helping me believe in what I was doing.

To The Plant Society family: you truly are a family. Nathan and I are so proud to have a team of hardworking individuals who not only support us, but each other.

To my partner, Nathan Smith: words can not sum up how amazing you are. This crazy journey is one we will always remember. One that I could not have done without you. There aren't many couples who could live and work together, but somehow it works, and I'm so thankful for that.

About the author

Jason Chongue is the author of *Plant Society* and the Creative Director of Melbourne- and Sydney-based design studio and store The Plant Society (www.theplantsociety.com.au/@theplantsocietyau). After having gained a wealth of experience working as a Melbourne-based architect and interior designer, Jason merged his passion for plants and design by establishing The Plant Society in 2016, focusing on designing with plants in small urban spaces.

Together with his partner, Nathan Smith, Jason leads and mentors a growing team at The Plant Society in their Melbourne and Sydney studios and stores. Jason and Nathan are involved in a vast range of plant projects across Australia, promoting positive and open conversations about gardening and greenery, not only indoors but in compact outdoor environments. Their focus on community and honest relationships has seen them work with various brands and in unique spaces, both designing with and looking after plants on a regular basis.

Since being established, The Plant Society has grown exponentially and has attracted a loyal following in Australia and globally. Jason regularly travels internationally to pass on his knowledge to aspiring plant enthusiasts in plant workshops.

PUBLISHED IN 2019 BY HARDIE GRANT BOOKS,
AN IMPRINT OF HARDIE GRANT PUBLISHING

HARDIE GRANT BOOKS (MELBOURNE)
BUILDING 1, 658 CHURCH STREET
RICHMOND, VICTORIA 3121

HARDIE GRANT BOOKS (LONDON)
5TH & 6TH FLOORS
52–54 SOUTHWARK STREET
LONDON SE1 1UN

HARDIEGRANTBOOKS.COM

ALL RIGHTS RESERVED. NO PART OF THIS PUBLICATION MAY BE REPRODUCED,
STORED IN A RETRIEVAL SYSTEM OR TRANSMITTED IN ANY FORM BY ANY MEANS,
ELECTRONIC, MECHANICAL, PHOTOCOPYING, RECORDING OR OTHERWISE, WITHOUT
THE PRIOR WRITTEN PERMISSION OF THE PUBLISHERS AND COPYRIGHT HOLDERS.

THE MORAL RIGHTS OF THE AUTHOR HAVE BEEN ASSERTED.

COPYRIGHT TEXT © JASON CHONGUE 2019
COPYRIGHT PHOTOGRAPHY © ARMELLE HABIB 2019
COPYRIGHT ILLUSTRATIONS © SHELLEY STEER 2019
COPYRIGHT DESIGN © HARDIE GRANT PUBLISHING 2019

 A catalogue record for this
book is available from the
National Library of Australia

GREEN

ISBN 978 1 74379 554 5

10 9 8 7 6 5 4 3 2 1

PUBLISHING DIRECTOR: JANE WILLSON
PROJECT EDITOR: ANNA COLLETT
EDITOR: KATE J. ARMSTRONG
DESIGN MANAGER: JESSICA LOWE
DESIGNER: ANDY WARREN
PHOTOGRAPHER: ARMELLE HABIB
ILLUSTRATOR: SHELLEY STEER
PRODUCTION MANAGER: TODD RECHNER
PRODUCTION COORDINATOR: MIETTA YANS

COLOUR REPRODUCTION BY SPLITTING IMAGE COLOUR STUDIO
PRINTED IN CHINA BY LEO PAPER PRODUCTS LTD.

SPECIAL THANKS TO AJAR @AJARFURNITURE HTTP://AJAR.COM.AU, LIGHTLY @LIGHTLYDESIGN WWW.LIGHTLY.COM.AU,
BUNGALOW TRADING CO @BUNGALOWTRADINGCO HTTPS://BUNGALOWTRADINGCO.COM.AU, SUSAN CHRISTIE @S.D.CHRISTIE
WWW.FORMANTICS.CO.NZ/, MELANIE MACILWAIN @MELANIE_MACILWAIN WWW.MELANIEMACILWAIN.COM, FORMAN ART AND FRAMING
@FORMANPICTUREFRAMING WWW.FORMANARTANDFRAMING.COM.AU, SBW @SBWAUSTRALIA WWW.SBWAUSTRALIA.COM.AU,
MARNIE GILDER @MARNIEGILDER WWW.MARNIEGILDER.COM, GRAZIA AND CO @GRAZIA_AND_CO WWW.GRAZIAANDCO.COM.AU
FOR GENEROUSLY PROVIDING PROPS FOR THE PHOTOSHOOT.